T0012663

CULTURE SMART!

ARGENTINA

THE ESSENTIAL GUIDE TO CUSTOMS & CULTURE

MARY GODWARD AND
ROBERT HAMWEE

KUPERARD

"The real voyage of discovery consists not in seeking new landscapes, but in having new eyes."

Adapted from Marcel Proust, *Remembrance of Things Past.*

ISBN 978 1 78702 336 9

British Library Cataloguing in Publication Data
A CIP catalogue entry for this book is available
from the British Library

First published in Great Britain
by Kuperard, an imprint of Bravo Ltd
59 Hutton Grove, London N12 8DS
Tel: +44 (0) 20 8446 2440
www.culturesmart.co.uk
Inquiries: publicity@kuperard.co.uk

Design Bobby Birchall
Printed in Türkiye by Elma Basim

ABOUT THE AUTHORS

MARY GODWARD was born in Buenos Aires and has lived in Argentina for most of her life. A specialist in cultural relations, she has designed and directed projects in education, science, arts, and literature for both public and private organizations. Before her retirement in 2019, Mary was Country Director for the British Council in Argentina for over 4 years. She now enjoys traveling with her family, sharing a *cafecito* with friends, researching her ancestors, and teaching English and Spanish to foreign students.

ROBERT HAMWEE was born and brought up in Argentina. He speaks six languages and has a decades-long career in international learning and development consulting that focuses on leadership, management, and cross-cultural communication. Today Robert lives in Norfolk, England, with his wife Sandra, their four dogs, and two rescue cats. Outside work Robert follows his many passions, among them music, which he writes and arranges, and conducts orchestras in major concert halls. A keen pilot, Robert will take to the skies whenever the opportunity arises.

CONTENTS

INTRODUCTION

Argentina is a country that embraces much more than gauchos, tango, and football. Unlike its Latin American neighbors, it has evolved in a distinctive way, and is quite different from the expectations many visitors have of a stereotypical Latin American destination.

The Argentinians have developed a style, a language, and a way of life that are all their own. They are a passionate, friendly, extroverted, and, particularly in Buenos Aires, vociferous people who have experienced the hardships of cruel economic downturns and hyperinflation of gargantuan proportions. For Argentinians there have also been golden eras, when traveling abroad was commonplace and, ironically, cheaper than staying at home.

Argentinians are stylish, sophisticated, and quite homogeneous—it is not the multicultural society we find in other Latin American countries. Neither very disciplined in their everyday life, nor great team players, they are, however, a nation of hardworking and resilient people whose character has been molded by external factors rather than driven by internal values.

The waves of immigrants that arrived in the twentieth century, mainly from Europe, brought with them a wealth of knowledge and culture that played a crucial role in the country's development of art, literature, and general lifestyle. Buenos Aires, with one of the world's largest opera houses, as well as museums and galleries, has produced writers and poets of distinction, and has gained a reputation as one of Latin America's great cultural centers.

After 1930 Argentina underwent a series of political upheavals, culminating in a coup in 1976 that brought one of the worst dictatorships in its history. The war with Britain in 1982 over the Falkland Islands, or Islas Malvinas, contributed to the government's own downfall and paved the way, albeit aided by a sad turn of events, for the restoration of democracy.

Still facing political and economic problems, the Argentinians today seem to have gained control of their own destiny. This, however, has been marred by a series of questionable economic policies and tense relationships with foreign investors, leading to pessimism about their government's ability to manage the ailing economy. The prolonged Covid-19 lockdowns resulted, as in many other countries, in closures and stagnation, from which Argentina has found it a challenge to recover. Despite these problems, Argentinians welcome visitors with open arms.

This book deals with the many facets of the Argentinian way of life. It has been designed to give you an insight into their social and business habits, culture, customs, and values. We hope to share with you our experiences of this great nation, which always seems to bounce back from adversity with unique, life-affirming joie de vivre.

Official Name	República Argentina	
Population	46 million	
Capital	Buenos Aires	(Short for "Puerto de Nuestra Señora Santa María del Buen Aire")
Main Cities	Buenos Aires (pop. 3 million, city only), Córdoba (pop. 1.62 million), Rosario (pop. 1.59 million), Mendoza (pop. 1.26 million)	
Area	1,068,302 sq. miles (2,766,890 sq. km)	Excl. islands in the South Atlantic and a portion of the Antarctic
Geography	Argentina is located on the Southern Cone of South America.	Bordering countries: Bolivia, Paraguay, Chile (divided by the Andes mountain range), Brazil, and Uruguay
Climate	Ranging from hot subtropical in the north to cold Antarctic in the south	
Population Density	17 inhabitants per sq. km	Despite a low pop. density overall, 92% of the pop. are concentrated in urban centers.
Language	Castellano	(Castilian Spanish)
Religion	The official religion is Catholicism.	Roman Catholic 62.9%, Evangelical 15.3%, None (includes atheist and agnostic) 18.9%, Judaism and Islam 1.5%, Other 1.4%.
National Holidays	Independence Day, July 9; Day of the May Revolution, May 25	

Government	Argentina is a federal republic with 23 provinces and 1 autonomous city (Buenos Aires). The president is head of state. Each presidential term lasts four years. There are two chambers: the Senate (Cámara de Senadores) representing the 23 provinces and the autonomous city of Buenos Aires, and the House of Representatives (Cámara de Diputados) representing the population on a proportional representation basis.	
Currency	The peso. There are 100 cents (centavos) to the peso.	Notes: 2, 5, 10, 20, 50, 100, 200, 500, and 1000 pesos. Coins: 1, 2, and 5 pesos and 1, 5, 10, 25, and 50 centavos
Media	Main newspapers include *Clarín* (popular daily), *La Nación* (conservative daily), *Cronica* (tabloid daily), *La Prensa* (Argentina's oldest newspaper). *Télam* is the state run news agency. *Infobae* is a popular online news portal.	Argentina's media is generally free from censorship, according to Freedom House. A measure of self-censorship may be employed in crime stories where the threat of violence is possible.
English Language Media	*Buenos Aires Herald*	*Buenos Aires Times*
Electricity	220 volts, 50 Hz	Two types of plugs: 2-pronged (rounded) in older buildings; 3-pronged (flat) in newer houses.
Internet Domain	.ar	
Telephone	Country code: 54	
Time	GMT -3	

CHAPTER ONE

LAND *&* PEOPLE

GEOGRAPHICAL SNAPSHOT

Argentina is not a land of palm trees and tropical beaches, as most images of South America seem to imply. Associating a Latin American country with skiing and cold winters as well as hot and humid summers might seem odd, but this is one of many aspects that make Argentina so exciting and unforgettable.

Argentina is the eighth-largest country in the world and the second-largest in South America (after Brazil), covering a distance of almost 2,300 miles (3,700 km) from its northernmost to southernmost points. As a result, it offers an outstanding variety of scenery, climate, and geographical features.

To the west, dividing Chile and Argentina, lies the Andes mountain range, extending all the way from the northwestern corner to the southern tip

Glacier Perito Moreno in Patagonia.

of the country. The Puna is a large plain that lies at an average of 10,499 feet (3,200 meters) above sea level on the northwestern corner of Argentina near the borders with Bolivia and Chile. As you go south along the Andes you'll reach the region of Cuyo, an area whose mountains are snowcapped throughout the year. Many passes are frequently blocked by heavy snowfalls during winter. It is in this area that you will find the 22,831-foot (6,959-meter) Mount Aconcagua, the highest peak in the Andes range, and indeed in South America.

Further south lies Patagonia, where the landscape features lakes, forests, and sharp mountain peaks near the Andes in the west, very reminiscent of an Alpine scene, and a vast semi-desert plain as you travel east toward the Atlantic Ocean. As you approach the southernmost tip of continental Argentina, on the way to Tierra del Fuego ("Land of Fire"), named after the fires lit by the Indigenous peoples of the region, you will find spectacular views of glaciers, including one of the world's largest, Glaciar Perito Moreno.

Nature and wildlife enthusiasts are spoiled for choice in Patagonia. Whales, penguins, and many species of birds are among the fauna of the area. Many initiatives have been put in place to safeguard the wildlife of the region, which is facing a rapid decline in numbers and in some cases the sad possibility of extinction.

THE REGIONS AND CLIMATE

Due to Argentina's great coverage in terms of latitude (a span of 34 degrees), different climates can be observed as one travels in a north–south direction. These range from hot subtropical in the northwest, close to the border with Bolivia, to freezing temperatures in the glacier regions of the south. Visitors are advised to bring the appropriate clothing for the regions and the season of their visit.

The Northwest

This is a mountainous region of hot climate and very colorful landscapes, mainly comprising the provinces

The multihued slopes of Quebrada de Humahuaca in Salta.

of Jujuy, Salta, La Rioja, Catamarca, Santiago del Estero, and Tucumán. It's an area of historic relics, old churches, and ruins of structures that were once part of the great Inca civilization.

The high plains of the Puna cover a vast area extending well into northwest Chile, southwest Bolivia, and southern Peru. It is made up of a series of plains, 9,843 to 11,483 feet (3,000 to 3,500 meters) high, separated by lower hills formed by intense volcanic activity. It has a hot climate, with temperatures soaring during the day but dropping sharply at night.

The Eastern Andes is where the famous *quebradas* lie, a series of colorful valleys that form one of the most important tourist attractions of the area. Among them is the famous Quebrada de Humahuaca, which was declared a UNESCO World Heritage Site in 2003.

The East and Northeast

Traveling east, you will find the subtropical forests of Formosa and Chaco, rich in flora and fauna and with a hot and humid climate. This is an area of large rivers, rich landscapes, and exuberant vegetation, home to many national parks and the famous Iguazú Falls.

The rivers Paraná and Uruguay run along the eastern and western borders of the provinces of

Iguazú Falls, Misiones.

Misiones, Corrientes, and Entre Ríos. These three provinces are known as Mesopotamia, a name that in Greek means "between rivers," echoing the Spanish translation of province Entre Ríos. The people that live here are cheerful, friendly, and hospitable, having developed their own style of language and music (*chamamé*), and share some characteristics with their Paraguayan neighbors. The work carried out by missionaries in the sixteenth and seventeenth centuries has left behind a legacy of historic Jesuit ruins, which today form a World Heritage area.

Cuyo

This region lies halfway down the country and is made up of the provinces Mendoza and San Juan, bordering Chile to the west and San Luis to the southeast of the region. Dominated by high peaks, snowcapped mountains, and rocky landscapes, its climate can be quite varied due to the influence of the Andes, with hot summers and freezing winters as one travels west. The province of Mendoza has gained a reputation as a producer of excellent wines. Most grapes (of European origin) have been grown in the region since the sixteenth century.

The park of Ischigualasto, or Valle de la Luna ("Valley of the Moon"), in the province of San Juan offers a quasi-surrealist lunar-like landscape. This and the bordering Talampaya National Park are famous for their fossils and a haven for paleontologists.

The moonlike landscape of Valle de la Luna Amarillo, in General Roca.

The Pampas

The region known as Pampa Húmeda ("Humid Pampa")
is the center of agricultural activity, having the richest
soil in the country. It comprises the provinces of
Buenos Aires, Santa Fe, and La Pampa. It is generally
flat, with two small areas of low hills in the regions of
Tandil and Ventana. A temperate climate predominates,
where temperatures can range from the mid-nineties
Fahrenheit (mid-thirties Celsius) during the hot and
humid summers (January to March) to just below
freezing in winter.

Laguna Esmeralda in Patagonian archipelago Tierra del Fuego.

The West and South

As one reaches Tierra del Fuego in the south, temperatures can easily reach 5°F (−15°C) in winter and climb to about 64°F (18°C) in summer. Ushuaia, its capital, is the second southernmost city in the world, after Puerto Williams in neighboring Chile.

To the west of the country, running along the Andes from the province of Mendoza, through Neuquén, Rio Negro, Chubut, and Santa Cruz, all the way down south to Tierra del Fuego, heavy snowfalls and sub-zero temperatures in winter provide the ideal

conditions for winter sports. It is here that Argentina's ski resorts can be found, ranging from important international centers to smaller local ones.

THE ARGENTINIANS: A VERY MIXED BAG

Many cultures have helped to shape Argentina's society into one that differentiates itself from the rest of Latin America. Spanish, Italian, German, French, British, and more recently Korean, Chinese, Paraguayan, Bolivian, Colombian, and Venezuelan immigrants have all found a home in Argentina. The extent to which these groups are represented varies in number, but they make up about 97 percent of the population.

On the other hand, Afro-Argentinians constitute a

Indigenous women with their children in Santa Victoria Este, in the city of Salta.

very small minority. Despite slavery having been no less prevalent in Argentina than in other countries until the early nineteenth century, the black community represents less than 1 percent of the overall population. The same applies to other ethnic minorities such as descendants of Indigenous peoples.

The Italians and Spanish

Argentina has witnessed great waves of immigrants throughout its history. The Spanish and Italians were by far the largest groups to seek new fortunes in the New World, and evidence of this is very strong in everyday life. A large proportion of surnames in Argentina are either Italian or Spanish; even local slang incorporates some Italian words. Unsurprisingly many of these communities have not developed in the same way as their European counterparts, the Italians perhaps remaining more Italian than their ancestors back home, and likewise the Spanish. This is possibly a result of being cut off from their roots and of not being exposed to common external factors that have molded other societies over the years. Currently, over eight hundred thousand Argentinians have Italian citizenship.

The first and second generations who arrived in Argentina still spoke their ancestors' language, and many of them spoke Spanish with a heavy accent, particularly the Galician community. As subsequent generations were born and educated in Argentina, and older generations passed away, their original languages would no longer be spoken. Typical Spanish names like González, Rodríguez, and Gómez are the most common surnames in Argentina. The Italians and Spanish brought with them strong Catholic sensibilities and a firm sense of family unity that to this day remains at the heart of Argentinian values.

The English, the Scots, and the Welsh

The small British community held an important place within Argentinian society in areas such as commerce, trade, and industry. The British community has retained a strong identity, although they are now well integrated into Argentinian society. They were instrumental in the development of Argentina's large railway network—the opportunities for employment and the skills required opened the doors to a wave of immigrants from Britain.

Left-hand Drive?

Although road traffic in Argentina drives on the right, trains still drive on the left—a legacy of British influence.

Despite a brief period of low popularity during the South Atlantic War in 1982, the Argentine-British community continues to be represented and respected across the country. It has grown over the years, with many settling in the capital and others opting for cities like La Cumbre in the province of Córdoba and Bariloche, in Río Negro.

Since the early nineteenth century, Scots, Welsh, and English have arrived on the coasts of the River Plate, establishing closely knit communities and founding schools, churches, hospitals, and businesses, many of which are still there to this day. Their influence is still evident in placenames such as Temperley, Wilde, and Hurlingham. Traditional private English schools are still favored by many as a paragon of good education.

Ceilidhs, bagpipes, and kilts are very much part of life for the Scottish community, who have continued to make their mark ever since the arrival of the first group of Scottish settlers in 1825. These traditions have been perpetuated through the St. Andrew's Society of the River Plate. Until the mid-1980s there was even a Harrods outlet in Buenos Aires, which although not officially a branch of the famous London store, had the same logo and corporate branding. Today, large shops like James Smart and Wrights are flagships of British influence in Argentina.

The Welsh arrived in Patagonia in 1865 and settled in the province of Chubut, mainly driven by the search for economic prosperity. They agreed to respect the laws of the country in exchange for land and respect for their own language and customs. Welsh tea houses, music, and Eisteddfods (poetry festivals), as well as the Welsh language, are still very much part of this community.

A Welsh Gorsedd ceremony, marking the start of an Eisteddfod festival in Gaiman.

On the sports front, soccer, rugby, hockey, golf, tennis, and polo are great icons of the British presence and are also among the sports in which Argentina has excelled.

A BRIEF HISTORY

The name Argentina derives from the word *argentum*, the Latin for silver. The name was coined by the Spanish conquistadores who believed there were large treasures in the area they discovered upon their arrival in the early sixteenth century. The River Plate is, in fact, a mistranslation of Río de la Plata, whose literal translation is "River of Silver," *plata* being the Spanish word for the precious metal. Argentina was a Spanish colony until it gained independence on July 9, 1816.

Early Inhabitants

Due to its vast area and marked variation in both climate and geographic features, many different Indigenous peoples inhabited Argentina in the early days. Much of the influence of these early inhabitants extended well beyond the borders of Argentina as we know them today. It is not surprising to see that so many centuries later, certain features and traditions are shared between those living in areas near the borders with Argentina's neighboring countries. These cultures and idiosyncrasies developed as a result of being faced with similar challenges, so commonalities can be found between Indigenous inhabitants of the Andean region of northwest Argentina stretching from the province of Córdoba all the way to the provinces of Salta and Jujuy, and their neighbors across the borders in the Bolivian, Chilean, and Peruvian Andes, where climate and landscape are very similar. Patagonia was mainly inhabited by the Tehuelches (also known as Patagones), Mapuches, Yamana (Yaganes), and the Selk'nam (Onas).

The Spanish Conquistadores

When the Spanish arrived on what is now Argentinian soil they found a land that was very sparsely populated. The estuary of the River Plate all the way up to Paraguay was inhabited by over fifteen different peoples, among them the Tupí-Guaraníes, Querandíes, and Mocoretás.

Argentina was officially "discovered" in 1516 by the Spanish navigator Juan Díaz de Solís, although many writers attribute its discovery to a Florentine explorer by the name of Amerigo Vespucci (Américo Vespucio in Spanish) in 1502. Vespucci was the first to claim that the newly discovered continent was not part of Asia (as originally thought); the mapmaker Martin Waldseemuller bestowed upon him, rather than Columbus, the title of discoverer of America and so named the continent after him. Vespucci died of malaria four years before Solís arrived at the estuary of the River Plate.

The "White King"

The quest to find a passage connecting the Atlantic and Pacific Oceans dates as far back as the days of the first conquistadores. Solís tried unsuccessfully to find a route by sailing up the River Plate, which he had initially called Mar Dulce ("Sweet Water Sea"), but it was not until four years later, in 1520, that Fernando de Magallanes (Magellan) achieved this by venturing south down the coast of Argentina and passing through the strait that bears his name. Solís was ambushed and killed by the Indigenous Querandíes (or Guaraníes) in 1516. Upon his death, the rest of his crew decided to return to Spain, not all of them reaching their homeland as many were shipwrecked or captured by locals.

Among those shipwrecked was a Portuguese

sailor by the name of Alejo García, who had found refuge on the island of Santa Catalina, off the coast of Brazil. Like many of his fellow sailors in the same predicament, he had heard from the Indigenous people on the nearby Brazilian coast of the existence of a king, a sovereign of immensely rich lands to the west. According to what he'd heard, the abundance of gold in this kingdom was such that even the houses were built with it. This monarch, according to the locals, was not of dark skin, but more like their conquerors. Thus the legend of the "White King" was born.

Spain's thirst for conquest of the Americas continued during the reign of Charles V (Charles I of Spain and later crowned Charles V, Holy Roman Emperor, in 1519). He sent his pilot-major, Sebastian Caboto (Cabot), to explore the River Plate; the fort of Sancti Spiritu that he founded in 1527, near modern Rosario, is considered to be the first Spanish settlement in Argentina.

The Birth of a Capital

In 1536, Pedro de Mendoza arrived at the River Plate. The purpose of his trip was threefold—to find the treasures of these new lands, to prevent Portuguese incursions into the territories, and to evangelize Indigenous people. In February of that year, he founded the city of Nuestra Señora Santa María del Buen Ayre, nowadays known as Buenos Aires. The name was given as an invocation of the Virgin Mary, a custom that had originated in Cagliari, Sardinia, which in those days belonged to Spain. Invocation of the Virgin for protection from the dangers of the sea was common practice among sailors of the Mediterranean.

The initial coexistence of the Amerindians and the conquistadores was a peaceful one, with Indigenous people supplying food in exchange for goods. This, however, did not last for long. The Amerindians became hostile and Mendoza was forced to sail up the coast of Brazil and the Paraná River in search of food. Mendoza's brother, Diego de Mendoza, remained behind, and he and those who stayed with him were attacked by a force of over one thousand. The confrontation that ensued, the Battle of Corpus Christi, resulted in the death of many Spaniards, including Diego de Mendoza.

The relative safety of the fortified city of Buenos Aires was to prove fatal. In June 1536, the city was besieged by thousands of Indigenous people. The Spanish were unable to obtain food and before long, starvation took its toll. One Ulrich Schmidl, a Bavarian soldier, later wrote, "People had nothing to eat and were starving. The situation was so terrible and hunger so disastrous that rats, mice, snakes, and lizards were not enough, and we eventually had to eat our own shoes and leather." Schmidl also added that there had even been cases of cannibalism among the unfortunate dwellers. The siege would eventually end when the

Amerindians set the city on fire. The Spanish were forced to retreat to their ships in order to survive.

Mendoza left Buenos Aires in 1537 and died en route back to Spain. The situation in the colony remained very unstable, mainly due to the hostility between the Indigenous people and the conquerors. Mendoza's successor, Domingo Martínez de Irala, decided to abandon the now besieged city and moved north to the city of Asunción (present capital of Paraguay) in search of the legendary lands of the White King.

Several cities were founded toward the mid-sixteenth century in three distinct waves. The earliest came from the more established Spanish colonies in the Alto Perú and founded most of what are now the most important cities in northwestern Argentina: Santiago del Estero, Londres, Tucumán, Córdoba, Catamarca, Salta, La Rioja, and Jujuy. The following wave came from Chile, founding the cities of Mendoza, San Juan, and San Luis. The third wave came from Asunción and founded the cities of Santa Fe, Corrientes, and Buenos Aires. This was the second and final establishment of Buenos Aires by Juan de Garay in 1580.

The seventeenth century witnessed further changes on the religious front, dominated by the intense activities of the Jesuits, mainly in the provinces of Córdoba, Corrientes, Chaco, Misiones (named after them), and the south of the province of Buenos

Aires, founding a further fifty-seven towns. In 1613 the Jesuits founded in Córdoba the first university in Argentina. They were expelled in 1767 by Charles III of Spain for reasons that to this day remain unclear. The Jesuits were, in fact, expelled from all Spanish territories, and the River Plate was no exception.

The Journey Toward Independence

By 1620 the entire River Plate region was under the administrative control of the Viceroyalty of Peru (Virreinato del Perú), and its colonization in the seventeenth century began to slow in comparison to the previous century. Buenos Aires became a buoyant commercial town and by the mid-1600s its population had grown to almost twenty thousand.

The size of the Viceroyalty of Peru was too great, and it was difficult to administer and defend. The growing importance of Buenos Aires as a commercial center and the potential threat posed by French and British expeditions to the coast of Argentina had forced Charles III of Spain to reassess the situation in the colonies. In 1776 the territories now roughly occupied by Argentina, Bolivia, Paraguay, and Uruguay were separated from Peru and the Viceroyalty of the River Plate (Virreinato del Río de la Plata) was created. Buenos Aires was to be the capital—this offered, among other benefits, easier access to Spain across the Atlantic.

In the late seventeenth century, Spain had started to lose its power as a great colonizing nation; at the same time, Great Britain gained power and was quickly establishing its supremacy around the world. Colonial expansion was a key factor in economic and political hegemony, which, according to the theories of the time, went hand in hand. This drove Britain to send a fleet to the River Plate on the erroneous premise that the colony was poorly defended; the colonized population, which was disgruntled with its government, would welcome the invaders with open arms. Both attempts by Britain to take control of the River Plate ended in failure, with the British forces defeated by locally raised militias.

The Spanish viceroy, Rafael de Sobremonte, exacerbated an already fragile political climate by abandoning Buenos Aires, leaving the city at the mercy of its invaders. He took with him the royal coffers and sought refuge in the city of Córdoba. This not only led to Sobremonte's political ruin but also acted as a catalyst to a growing wish for independence on the part of many settlers.

Events in Europe, particularly as a result of the Napoleonic Wars and an already discredited colonial government, provided the colonists with an opportunity to step up their fight for independence. In May 1810, representatives of Buenos Aires (the municipal council or *cabildo*) set up a provisional government that would act directly on the king's behalf, making the viceroy's role redundant. The war for independence would last for another six years; until then the country would be plunged into a series of battles between those loyal to the Spanish crown and those supporting the popular movement for independence. Among the heroes of the war for independence, General José de San Martín is probably one of the most famous. With his five-thousand-strong cavalry regiment, sixteen thousand mules, and sixteen hundred horses (of which only 511 survived), he crossed the Andes and was instrumental in achieving independence for Chile and Peru. This feat of Herculean proportions has made San Martín one of the most venerated military heroes in Argentinian history.

On July 9, 1816, the Congress of Tucumán (Congreso de Tucumán) declared the independence of the United Provinces of South America (Provincias Unidas de América del Sur)—fourteen in total—and appointed a popular government represented by a junta, which drew up the first constitution establishing a centralized government in 1819. The ensuing years would be a period of anarchy fueled by political rivalry and the search for political stability.

Turmoil and Prosperity

Peace was restored in 1820, but the formation of a stable government remained an unresolved issue. In 1825 the neighboring empire of Brazil went to war against Argentina, as a result of disputed sovereignty claims over the territory known as the Banda Oriental ("Eastern Strip").

In 1826 the name of the United Provinces of the River Plate, adopted a year earlier, was abandoned in favor of the current name of Argentina. In 1828 the war with Brazil came to an end, and the disputed territory of the Banda Oriental gained its independence, adopting its present name of Uruguay.

No sooner had peace been restored than new upheavals came to dominate the political scene, culminating in the dictatorship of Juan Manuel de Rosas. As governor of the Province of Buenos Aires from 1835 to 1852, he had managed to consolidate friendly relationships with the other provinces, thus gaining popular support. In no time he extended his authority over the rest of the provinces, quashing any opposition. It was during this period that the British occupied the Falkland Islands/ Islas Malvinas for the first time.

Rosas was defeated in 1852 by a group of

A portrait of Juan Manuel de Rosas from 1840.

revolutionaries headed by former governor of the
Province of Entre Ríos, Justo Jose de Urquiza. The
following year, a federal constitution (based on the US
Constitution) was drawn up, with Urquiza becoming
the president of Argentina.

This was to be a temporary solution as Buenos Aires,
refusing to abide by the new constitution, declared its
independence from the rest of the provinces in 1854. In
1859 its situation became untenable, and a vanquished
Buenos Aires agreed to become part of the new
federation. Despite the political turmoil, it was an age
of prosperity for commerce as a result of new shipping
treaties signed with Great Britain, France, and the
United States. The constitution of 1853 also declared
the abolition of slavery in Argentina.

The end of the war of the Triple Alliance (Brazil,
Argentina, and Uruguay) against Paraguay in 1870
heralded a period of relative normality for Argentina.
In 1880, Buenos Aires was declared the federal capital
of the Argentine Republic. From then on, the political
arena would be dominated by two groups, the radicals
and the conservatives, who continue to fight for power
to this day.

From 1880, Argentina entered an era of prosperity,
establishing itself as one of the richest nations in the
world, aided by large waves of immigration. Agriculture,
the railways, and industry in general flourished during
this period. It was a time of relative peace with little
social unrest, which would last for almost half a century.

The Right to Choose

By the beginning of the twentieth century, Argentina was one of the world's richest countries. The population had grown substantially, partly as a result of the large numbers of European immigrants who, attracted by its prosperity, had come in search of better opportunities. In 1912 Roque Sáenz Peña sanctioned the electoral law that guaranteed universal and compulsory male suffrage from age eighteen by secret ballot.

During the First World War, Argentina's neutrality strengthened its ties with the United States, both politically and economically. This continued during the presidency of Hipólito Yrigoyen of the Radical Party (Partido Radical), elected in 1916 and reelected in 1928.

After the first military coup in 1930, twentieth-century Argentina was to be dominated by military governments, with brief interludes of civil democracy.

Hipólito Yrigoyen, pictured here in 1926.

The Birth of Nationalism

The leaders of the military coup of 1943 had claimed as their mission the eradication of the fraud and administrative corruption that had become prevalent in the higher echelons of government. Under the presidency of General Pedro Ramírez, all political activity would be banned until the new government's aims were accomplished. Behind all this was a looming fear that the government would abandon its position of neutrality and undertake fascist activities.

Argentina's independent political standpoint during the Second World War led to the weakening of its position internationally. In 1940, President Ortiz declared Argentina's neutrality, a policy that would later be abandoned by his successors, Ramon Castillo and Pedro Ramírez. After the Japanese attack on Pearl Harbor in December 1941, Argentina and Chile were the only two American countries that refused to sever ties with the Axis powers.

This policy led to the virtual economic isolation of Argentina by the United States, which forced Argentina's government to reassess its position and to sever diplomatic relations with Japan and Germany in 1944. Fearing that Ramírez, under pressure from the United States, would declare war against Germany, a military junta forced him out of office. This new government, despite the change in foreign policy initiated by Ramírez, was accused by the United States of supporting Germany and of sympathizing with the Nazi cause.

It was not until March 1945, when the Allied victory in Europe was a foregone conclusion, that Argentina declared war against Germany and Japan.

A key figure of the new regime was Juan Domingo Perón, a charismatic nationalist-populist who was to dominate Argentina's political scene for years to come. The Argentinian people had lived under military rule for too long and there was great discontent among the working class, who demanded better pay and working conditions. The presidency of Perón from 1946 to 1955 was characterized by a rise in popular movements and support for and by the working class (the Peronist or Justicialista Party). Juan and his astute wife, Eva (Evita), portrayed themselves as defenders of the popular cause and supporters of social welfare programs and trade unions, but all at the expense of the country's economy. Argentina's people had little welfare and many of them felt they were victims of an oligarchy that was becoming increasingly

General Juan Domingo Perón.

María Eva Duarte de Perón (Evita) in 1948.

powerful at their expense. Perón and Evita homed in on these feelings of discontent. When Eva died in 1952, aged 33, she was greatly mourned.

Perón grew more autocratic as the economic situation deteriorated. His failed attempt to build a corporatist state and to secularize a staunchly Catholic country created a rift between the Church and government that led not only to his excommunication by the Vatican, but to the end of his administration following a coup in 1955 led by General Leonardi. Perón fled to Spain, and Leonardi was later replaced by General Aramburu, who would remain in power until 1958. Aramburu was eventually assassinated by left-wing guerillas in May 1970.

Perón made a further dent in Argentina's reputation by allowing Nazi war criminals to enter the country, where they started new lives under new identities. Among these were mass murderers Josef Mengele, Walter Kutschmann, Klaus Barbie, and Adolf Eichmann, who was seized by the Israeli secret service in 1960 and smuggled out of the country to stand trial in Jerusalem.

Arturo Frondizi was elected president of Argentina in the 1958 ballot. His victory was secured after Perón (now in exile in Venezuela) ordered that the banned Peronist party should support him. Frondizi's term was fraught with economic difficulties and was closely scrutinized by the armed forces, who were not keen on once again handing over power to a civilian government. Frondizi's refusal to break ties with Cuba and his handling of Argentina's domestic politics eventually led to his resignation.

There was an unsuccessful attempt by the armed forces to sabotage the 1963 elections. They feared that a victory on behalf of the Peronist movement (although banned from all political activity) would plunge the country into total chaos. Perón yet again issued orders for support to be given to two candidates who were consequently excluded from the electoral process. The Radical Party, headed by Arturo Illia, won the elections, but after only three years was ousted in a coup led this time by General Juan Carlos Onganía.

For the next six years Argentina was to be ruled by military governments who continued to sow the seeds of discontent among the population. This gave rise to a series of left-wing guerrilla groups (Montoneros, FAR, ERP), many of them middle-class Catholic youths who felt they were being supported by Perón.

Confrontations between the armed forces and

guerrilla groups, kidnappings, and growing violence, coupled with high inflation and strikes, forced General Alejandro Lanusse to lead the country toward a democratic solution, promising elections in 1973 in the belief that only Perón could restore order.

1,035 Days of Chaos

Hector Cámpora won the 1973 elections as the Peronist candidate. One month after the new president took over, and after almost twenty years in exile in Spain, Juan Domingo Perón returned to Argentina. Two million people awaited his arrival in the streets leading to the airport in an event that was marred by an armed confrontation between right- and left-wing factions of the Peronist movement, resulting in thirteen deaths and about two hundred wounded. Cámpora was eventually forced to resign. After winning over 60 percent of votes, almost thirty years after he first took power, Perón became president of Argentina once more, with his new wife Maria Estela Martínez de Perón (Isabel) as vice president.

Perón's tenure was to last only a few months, until his death in July 1974. Isabel Perón took over as president, leading the country through a period rife with corruption, violence, terrorism, and political and economic chaos.

In March 1976 a military junta ousted Isabel Perón, ending 1,035 days of civilian government, and she eventually returned to Spain. The commander-in-chief of the army, General Jorge Rafael Videla, took over the presidency of Argentina, suspending all constitutional rights and political activity. This dictatorship took on as its main responsibility the eradication of all political insurgency and terrorism, mainly at the hands of the left-wing Montoneros guerrillas, and set about restoring "peace" by means of extreme repression that resulted in the death and disappearance of thousands of people.

While exact figures have not been agreed upon, subsequent investigations found that at least eight thousand people disappeared without trial during this so-called "dirty war." (Upper estimates put the figure as high as thirty thousand.) One sector of society, perhaps the more affluent one, had been living in fear of left-wing terrorist kidnappings and murders, and for many this purge seemed to be a necessary evil—but it resulted

Swearing in of President Jorge Rafael Videla in 1976.

in the whole population living in fear of a government that knew no bounds when it came to human rights. Both the innocent and the guilty fell prey to raids, arrests, and death.

By the early 1980s terrorism had been eradicated. Order had been restored, but at an inhumane price, and Argentina was now led by a military government that was unpopular at best and hated at worst by the vast majority of the population. Any sense of national pride had vanished, and Argentina's image was once again tarnished.

The South Atlantic War and the Restoration of Democracy

One of the presidents of this period of military rule in Argentina was General Leopoldo Galtieri. Faced with political opposition, an increase in activity by the trade unions, and an unhealthy economy, Galtieri decided to occupy and reclaim the Falkland/Malvinas Islands in April 1982. The defeat of Argentina in this conflict sealed the fate of military rule in Argentina.

Sovereignty over the Falklands/Malvinas had been an issue for more than a century. Claims of sovereignty had been made by both Britain and Argentina, and although the matter had never been resolved there had been a peaceful coexistence, with the Kelpers (the inhabitants of the islands) using Argentinian mainland facilities and regular flights to and from the mainland. The junta's original intention had been to enter into an armed conflict with Chile over a stretch of land in the Beagle

Strait. This never happened—the fact that the Chileans were only next door and were well armed probably served as a good deterrent. Britain, on the other hand, was far away and Argentina launched an attack on the assumption that Britain, being so distant and probably unconcerned about two small islands in the South Atlantic, would not retaliate. This proved to be a costly mistake.

On March 31, 1982, the people of Buenos Aires took to the Plaza de Mayo to demonstrate against Galtieri and the government, only to be met with fierce repression from the police and the army. Two days later, on April 2, they congregated with great euphoria to hail Galtieri as a hero for the invasion of the islands.

The government thought that it had achieved the patriotic unity so long desired and that this would help to clear Argentina's name after years of repression. Argentinians of all sectors of society, including many people radically opposed to the government, agreed that the islands should be Argentinian. Support for this cause became the norm, and those not in favor were branded as pro-British and enemies of the country.

By June, however, Argentina had suffered a terrible defeat at the hands of the British. Many young conscripts had been sent to fight against what was one of the best-trained professional armies in the world. Argentinian pride had been hurt like never before; even though foreign reports on the progress of the war had been banned, the outcome was clear weeks before the end of the conflict. Again people took to the streets, but the mood this time was very different.

Faced with total loss of credibility, low morale, inflation of over 200 percent, poor salaries, and a discredited armed forces, Galtieri was replaced by General Reynaldo Bignone, who vowed to be the last military president of Argentina. Bignone legalized political activity. In 1983, Raúl Alfonsín won the elections as head of the Radical Party, whose government eventually brought to trial the members of the past juntas, including those responsible for the invasion of the islands, charging them with human rights abuses. Argentina's economy was still ailing and would not recover for a few years to come.

Carlos Menem of the Peronist Party won the elections in 1989 and again in 1995. This was the first time in over half a century that power in Argentina was handed from one elected government to another. Menem's first presidency was characterized by a period of political stability and prosperity driven by a program of liberal economic policies in the hands of his Minister of Economy, Domingo Cavallo. It was during this period that a one-to-one parity with the US dollar was established.

However, corruption and administrative fraud slowly led the country to the brink of economic collapse. Menem's successor, Fernando de la Rúa of the Radical Party, found the national coffers virtually empty. Massive unemployment and hunger among the population led to the ransacking and looting of food outlets. This forced de la Rúa to take extreme and painful measures. Prompted by a run on the banks, he issued a decree limiting the withdrawal of funds. Sadly, the damage had already been done—over one billion dollars had been taken out of the country. In an unprecedented series of events, the population took to the streets and were met by harsh repression at the hands of the authorities. De la Rúa finally bowed to popular demand and resigned, leaving behind a crippled economy and a national industry in a state of decay.

De la Rúa's successor, Néstor Kirchner, faced the daunting task of getting the economy back on its feet, and the year 2004–5 witnessed a slow yet assuring improvement. Argentina had bounced back time and again from economic and political adversity. However, any sustainable economic recovery was to be short-lived. In 2007 Cristina Fernández de Kirchner took over the presidency from her husband after winning over 54 percent of the vote in the general elections. Argentina once again entered a period of sluggish growth and increasing inflation.

In 2015, following President Kirchner's unsuccessful attempt to amend the constitution to allow her to run for a third term, Argentina went to the polls once more amid a return to social, economic, and political uncertainty. This time the opposition, under the leadership of Mauricio Macri, won the election. He tried to implement market-oriented policies, but his efforts were crippled by a lack of majority in Congress. In the 2019 elections he was defeated by the Frente de Todos (Everyone's Front), led by

Alberto Fernández and Cristina Kirchner, who was voted back into office as vice president. Although President Fernández had promised to jump-start production and restore social programs aimed at curbing hunger and poverty, the economy continued to deteriorate, with inflation reaching 94.8 percent in 2022. In December 2022, a court sentenced Vice President Cristina Kirchner to six years in jail for corruption and banned her from public office for life. With presidential elections looming on the horizon, her supporters considered the sentence to be politically motivated.

GOVERNMENT AND POLITICS

Argentina is a federal republic divided into twenty-three provinces and Buenos Aires, the federal capital. Its constitution was modeled on that of the United States, and as in many similar republics the executive power is held by the president, alongside the legislative and judicial powers. The constitution is still that which was drawn up in 1853, although it has been subject to subsequent revisions. The latest of these, in 1994, allows the president to be reelected once and shortens the term of office from six to four years.

Legislative power lies in the hands of the Congress, made up of the House of Representatives (Cámara de Diputados), representing the population, and the Senate (Cámara de Senadores), representing the twenty-three provinces and the federal capital.

For the last sixty years the political arena has been dominated by two major parties, the Partido Radical (Radical Party) and the Partido Justicialista (Justicialist Party), the legacy of the old Peronist Party. Juntos por el Cambio (Together for Change), an alliance between the Radical Party and Mauricio Marci's followers, is the first strong political opposition to emerge in Argentina in many years.

THE ECONOMY

Argentina is a country with a huge wealth of natural resources, including oil, gas, and minerals. With over 32 million hectares of arable land yielding more than 145 million tons of cereals and oleaginous crops, it is still a country where agriculture provides the keystone to the economy and is the largest source of revenue. The main crops are wheat, barley, sunflower, maize, soy, and sorghum. Argentina's cattle head count stands at over 53 million, providing the economy with a generous supply of meat, dairy, and raw materials for the textile industry.

Industry has made rapid gains in Argentina; of these, food and beverages account for one third of the country's output. Chemical industries, vehicles, oil refineries, machinery, and the production of base metals represent another third.

However, over the last few years the economy has suffered and output has fallen as a result of the government's economic policies, including restrictions on imports and non-payment of creditors and investment funds. Argentina's seemingly uncompromising position has affected the government's credibility, and it has been faced with potential sanctions from the IMF due to non-compliance with agreements to implement fiscal and economic policies.

The consequences of failing economic policies are evident in Argentina in the form of increased inequality and poverty. Outbreaks of social unrest such as roadblocks and demonstrations are not unusual, particularly in Buenos Aires. These have become part of the landscape for Porteños (the capital city's inhabitants), who find a way to continue with their lives as normal.

COVID-19

The first Covid-19 case in Argentina was detected in early March 2020. The newly elected government acted swiftly and took bold decisions, imposing a comprehensive lockdown that lasted for eight long months, with schools reopening in November and restrictions still in place until the end of the year. The lockdowns were strictly enforced. In the early months exercise and dog walking were not allowed, and commercial flights into the country were banned for seven months. Despite these measures, which were widely accepted by the population, the upward trend in cases continued, particularly in the more informal settlements in the city of Buenos Aires and the greater metropolitan area. Other than lockdowns and social distancing, successful national vaccination campaigns played an important role in reducing the number of cases and deaths. As of January 2023, the World Health Organization reported an overall total of over 10 million cases and 130,249 fatalities in Argentina. José Miguel Vivanco from Human Rights Watch reported that Argentina's response to Covid-19 was "marred by a violent police response towards people accused of breaking the rules."

Dismissals were forbidden during the pandemic from March 2020 to April 2021, in spite of which unemployment reached 11 percent. Rents were frozen and evictions for non-payment were suspended. Welfare to poor families increased, alongside the number of minimum wage workers and activity within the informal economy. During the strictest stages of lockdown the government subsidized 50 percent of salaries for 2 million workers in private companies. Zero rate credits were made available for the self-employed as well as credit guarantees for bank loans to small- and medium-sized companies (SMEs).

By late 2022, the use of facemasks (*barbijos*) was no

longer compulsory at schools, in enclosed spaces, or on public transport. Economic activity has recovered faster than expected and, by mid-2022, Argentina's GDP was 7.5 percent above pre-pandemic levels.

As in other countries, some things in Argentina have changed forever as a result of the pandemic. For example, numerous companies that were already struggling in the challenging economic climate that preceded the pandemic did not survive the lockdowns. Sectors particularly harmed by the pandemic and the restrictions were hospitality and construction. With forty-one thousand closures, SMEs suffered the most.

In many ways, Covid-19 also forced people, private companies, and the government to more readily embrace the digital world. Working from home, online shopping, digital payments, and video conferencing, even for medical appointments, have now become a part of everyday life in Argentina.

MAJOR CITIES

Buenos Aires
The capital and largest city in Argentina, with a population of just under 15 million, including the federal capital and greater Buenos Aires, accounts for over one-third of Argentina's population. The capital itself had a population of 3.1 million in 2023. Built along the banks of the River Plate, it is the main entrance into

Argentina, a dynamic and vibrant city of imposing architecture, broad, tree-lined avenues, theaters, cinemas, galleries, bookshops, cafés, and a magnificent opera house. Buenos Aires has been deservedly called the Paris of South America.

The wide range of architectural styles—from old Hispanic colonial buildings to magnificent neoclassical palaces and modern glass and steel designs—places Buenos Aires in a league of its own. Its sophistication is reminiscent of Paris or Madrid, yet it preserves a strong element of local tradition in its music (tango), its language (with its distinctive accent), and its vociferous and friendly people (the Porteños).

Like many large cities, Buenos Aires is a fast-moving place. It is the seat of the government and of many international corporations. In 1978, despite controversy about the politics of the military government, Argentina hosted the football World Cup, with Buenos Aires as the focal point for the event. This had a deep impact on the infrastructure of the city and its attitude to visitors. Today the capital has a lot to offer, from its elegant shopping streets to food of epicurean standards. Plaza de Mayo, San Telmo, La Boca and Palermo, and the stylish area of La Recoleta show different facets of the city and should not be missed. From a cultural perspective, the Museo de Bellas Artes (Fine Arts Museum) holds regular exhibitions of international caliber, and the Palacio Errázuriz houses the museum of decorative arts. MALBA, the Buenos Aires museum for Latin American art, defined as "one of the cornerstones of the city's cultural life" by Fodor's Travel, has an excellent permanent collection and hosts some of the best temporary exhibitions in town.

Music lovers will be able to choose from a wide range of genres, from the local tango shows to excellent jazz at the traditional Café Tortoni. The Opera House is one of the finest in the world, featuring a roster of international artists during its opera and concert season in a magnificent auditorium with first-rate acoustics.

Between 1880 and 1920 the face of Buenos Aires changed profoundly. Urban growth and changes in technology were accompanied by social and cultural transformation as a result of the numbers of immigrants from Europe that arrived in Argentina. More than 4 million people entered the country between 1857 and 1920. These people brought with them cultures, values, and norms that have played a key role in Argentinian society up to the present day.

Porteños are stylish and sophisticated, and their mannerisms, accent, customs, and diverse roots set them apart from the rest of the population.

Córdoba

Located in the center of the country, Córdoba is the second-largest city in Argentina with a population of just under 1.4 million. Popularly known as the "City of Bells," a nickname inspired by the large number of churches, it offers a wide range of museums and green

Iglesia del Sagrado Corazon (Sacred Heart Church) or Church of the Capuchins, Córdoba.

spaces, such as the Parque Sarmiento. The Indigenous Comechingones created some of the greatest pictorial relics in Argentina here, having left over one thousand paintings and etchings in many caves.

Córdoba was host to important and sometimes bloody political events in the twentieth century, and has continued to be a focal point for union activities.

The Cordobeses are friendly, determined, and are known for their great sense of humor. They also possess a very distinctive accent that is almost musical.

CHAPTER TWO

VALUES & ATTITUDES

FAMILY FIRST

Argentina, like most Latin American and Mediterranean nations, is a country of strong family values. Despite changes in social norms, the family remains a solid institution. It's normal even today for children to live with their parents until they get married, although the custom of leaving home after reaching a certain age is increasing rapidly. The main determining factor is a financial one, as property is expensive and until a few years ago mortgages were not commonplace; even now, when mortgages are available, not many can afford them.

City dwellers lead a life not dissimilar to that of the inhabitants of any big city, but the difference between life in Buenos Aires and the quieter rural life of the remote areas of the country could not be greater.

Family gatherings (particularly on Sundays) are the norm; sometimes this even extends to uncles, aunts, grandparents, and cousins, so these events can become very lively. Children come first and are welcome in most places. They are looked after, brought up, and educated to their parents' best ability and constantly encouraged to compete and succeed. In turn, it's not unusual for the younger generation to look after their elderly parents; in many cases, parents move in with their children. There is a constant quest to maintain this family unity. It is still common practice for young adults to go to university near their home when possible, and parental approval for many things is sought. It is these strong family ties that have helped many survive harsh economic climates and political instability.

For Argentina, the years since the reestablishment of democratic government in 1983 has been a period characterized by a feeling of having to make up for lost time. The last two decades in particular have brought about many changes. For example, fewer people today get married, and those who do so get married later, on average at age 34, which is nearly six years older than it was in 1990. Today more are also comfortable opting to simply live together, with or without a civil union.

The number of single mothers has risen, perhaps as a result of an increased ability on the part of women to gain financial independence and escape conflictive or violent marriages. By 2023, women were also having one-third fewer children than a decade earlier, and were having them at a later age.

La Gauchada

This is a term used to refer to a special favor. It represents an attitude, a friendly way to request help when asking someone to do something outside their normal duties.

PROUD TO BE ARGENTINIAN

National pride extends to many, but not all, areas—food, clothes, way of life, and, of course, football. This is particularly the case during World Cup matches, when the country seems to come to a standstill and

Fans in Buenos Aires celebrate Argentina's World Cup 2022 soccer victory.

then explode in celebration when the national team wins. Over 5 million people took to the streets to greet the Argentina squad after they won the World Cup in 2022: a moment of jubilation in the aftermath of the pandemic and a struggling economy.

Areas such as politics and the economy are not something Argentinians tend to boast about. Patriotism as a value has not really existed in Argentina until recently. Unstable economic situations and a general mistrust of incompetent governments have made people adopt a justifiably selfish attitude, putting themselves first, irrespective of whether it is good for the country or not.

Argentinians tend to be forgiving and fair. The jingoism that was inculcated in them during the military dictatorship, and that led to great animosity between Britain and Argentina during the South Atlantic War, has, fortunately, not survived. However, its governments have tended to use the issue of sovereignty over the islands as a red herring in an attempt to distract people's attention from more domestic issues. Patriotism and national pride are mostly only visible when instigated by an external event, such as an armed conflict or an international sporting victory. When Argentina hosted the World Cup in 1978, and won it, many took to the streets in celebration, even as others were quietly disappearing in the so-called "dirty war."

DISCIPLINE AND HONESTY

Discipline is not a national trait and it's not something Argentinians are in denial about. If given the option of bending the rules slightly to their own advantage, most will take it. If confronted with their actions, they will admit fault but shrug. Argentinians are basically honest people who for many years have been at the mercy of dishonest governments, high taxation, and crippling laws and this has resulted in a cynical approach to life, and particularly to politics, and as a result people often try to find a way to cut corners.

Who you know is still more important than what you know, and leverage (*palanca)* is still very much in use when it comes to looking for a job. Contacts will in many cases count more than skill and competency, though this is more prevalent in the public sector.

The private sector prides itself on being professional and adequately staffed when it comes to skills and qualifications. Indeed, Argentinian professionals spend up to six years in college, combining their studies with full-time work in most cases. Discipline may not be their strength, but a strong work ethic and tenacity are.

Bribery (*coima*), a result of poor pay among civil servants and an inefficient bureaucratic apparatus, is widespread in certain sectors. Policemen, traffic wardens, and civil servants have been known to accept bribes. It isn't wise to try and engage in any, though; if faced with a potential problem with the authorities you're better off contacting your embassy or consulate.

Loopholes in the system will be exploited with a self-gratifying sense of having outsmarted the rest. This attitude ("*viveza criolla*" or "*avivada*") has given the Argentinians a bad reputation among other Latin American countries, who sometimes see them as supercilious and arrogant.

COMMUNITY AND INDIVIDUALISM

Argentinians are very sociable but in general don't have a strong community spirit, outside that generated by the church they might attend. Working as a team or in a group can therefore be a challenge, as each member will probably try (albeit not maliciously) to outsmart the rest, and hidden agendas will almost certainly play a part.

As things stand, the education system is not designed to produce team players, but stars. This is evident in politics, business, and even the arts, where merit is ascribed normally to one individual rather than to a group of people.

Individualists by nature, perhaps due partly to a permanent mistrust of their political leaders, Argentinians have developed an attitude of putting themselves first at the expense of the collective. Collaborative accomplishments are not often recognized, and people will tend to single out an individual to give credit to for an achievement—or to point the finger of blame at, should things go wrong.

This doesn't mean that all Argentinians are indifferent to their community or their country. There are groups, notably the younger generations, who are developing a stronger sense of community. Protecting the environment and their national heritage, and having a sense of responsibility for looking after their country, are values that are slowly being embraced.

THE CHURCH AND RELIGION

Argentina is a staunchly Catholic country where abortion was prohibited until 2021 and divorce was not merely frowned upon but illegal until 1987. Despite a growing number of people who define themselves as "non-religious," approximately 63 percent still identify as Roman Catholic, according to the National Survey of Religious Beliefs and Attitudes. Through the uncertainty of political and economic upheaval, the Church provided solace, and in many cases food and shelter.

Argentinians can be pious, but not to the extent found in other Catholic countries. With the arrival of democracy, people have become much more open in the expression of their feelings and opinions. For example, attitudes to sexuality have changed, and the Argentinians have embraced liberal views on sexual matters that would once have been considered reprehensible by those adhering to strictly Catholic values. (See pages 66–69 for more.)

Attending Sunday mass is commonplace and, by and large, Argentinians are observant of the Catholic traditions of their Italian and Spanish ancestors.

Names also reflect the country's Catholic heritage, particularly the use of the names of Mary and Joseph.

The San Francisco Church, located in Salta.

Female names like María are frequently used as second names for men, and by the same token the traditionally male name José can be used as a woman's middle name. So for example, María José is a woman's name, while José María is a man's name.

The pilgrimage from Buenos Aires to Luján is perhaps the largest of its kind in Argentina. The fifty-mile walk takes place every October and often sees over a million devout Argentinian Catholics taking part.

In general terms, Argentines welcomed the election of Jorge Bergoglio as Pope Francis in 2013, and many admired him for his simple tastes. A decade later, opinions today are more divided, however. For the conservative, he is considered too progressive, and for the progressive, too conservative. He has also come under fire for what initially appeared to be sympathetic views toward Peronist politicians, and the fact that he has visited fifty-eight countries, including most in South America, but not yet Argentina!

WORK ETHIC

Argentinians are, by and large, hardworking individuals who until recently were not accustomed to a very competitive environment. The arrival of technology, the globalization of the economy, and the resulting quest for cutting costs and maximizing profits, particularly during adverse economic periods, have created a culture of aggressive marketing tactics and diverse working practices.

Multinational organizations have brought with them new approaches and a more meritocratic work ethic. The older generation has sometimes found this hard to come to terms with, being from a hierarchical society where length of service weighs more heavily than achievement when it comes to seniority within an organization. This new work ethic is slowly superseding the old way of doing things.

Argentinian society generally has a low level of tolerance for uncertainty. In an effort to minimize or reduce uncertainty, strict rules, laws, policies, and regulations are adopted and implemented with varying degrees of success. Individual Argentinians have a tendency to control everything in order to eliminate or avoid uncertainty. As a result, they will rarely embrace or even accept change and tend to be averse to risk-taking.

ATTITUDES TOWARD GENDER AND SEXUALITY

As in many cultures where men have traditionally been the breadwinners and women have largely been responsible for running the house and looking after the children, the deep-rooted concept of

Participants at the Pride march in Buenos Aires.

machismo is still evident in Argentina today. That said, the role of women in Argentinian society has changed dramatically in recent years, particularly in urban areas, and women are now influential in the fields of politics, business, the arts, and science.

In the early 1970s, a series of feminist movements began to establish a change in the role of women in Argentina. Their work and emancipation was hindered by the arrival of the dictatorship in 1976, but their presence was still visible. Since then women have become key players in the day-to-day development of Argentina's society. The ousting of president Fernando de la Rúa was, in fact, initiated by women—they took to the streets en masse, banging their pots in protest, a tactic that proved much more effective than the use of armed force.

The Madres and Abuelas de Plaza de Mayo have made their cause heard all over the world. They exerted pressure on the government to release details of the whereabouts of their missing children and grandchildren, who were among the thousands who disappeared at the hands of the military government.

In more recent times, grassroots feminist movements such as Ni Una Menos (Not One [woman] Less), have pushed women's rights to the top of the political agenda and have helped to instigate positive change. The Marea Verde (Green Wave) movement, also initiated in Buenos Aires, has seen the *pañuelo verde* (green scarf) become the symbol worn in support of reproductive rights across Latin America.

When it comes to higher education in Argentina, 59 percent of students in 2023 were women, though they accounted for 51 percent of the population and one third of Argentina's workforce. As a result, the biggest rise in female employment has been in the specialized fields of science and technology. However, even in these fields glass ceilings persist, alongside salary differentials of about 25 percent between men and women who perform the same task. These are slowly giving way to an egalitarian approach, perhaps influenced by foreign companies who take a different view of what working women are owed. The assertive behavior and tenacity of Argentinian women continue to act as strong catalysts for ongoing change.

Argentina was the first country in Latin America to legalize same-sex marriage, including adoption rights, in 2010. This was followed in 2012 by a Gender Identity Law, allowing transgender Argentinians to change their legal genders and names. Flor de la V, the first transgender person in Argentina to have her name and gender changed on her government-issued ID, is a well-known actress, television personality, comedian, and vedette. She is also an active member of the LGBTQ community. More recently, Argentina recognized non-binary gender identities in its national identification cards and passports, giving individuals the option of having their sex marked with an "X."

Despite the introduction of these previously unprecedented legal protections, attitudes toward a person's right to openly express their sexuality are not homogenous across Argentina. As in other countries, attitudes in the larger cities, particularly Buenos Aires, are different to those in smaller towns, where more conservative views prevail. Overall support for same-sex marriage has grown by 25 percent in the last ten years.

Buenos Aires has been called the most gay-friendly Latin American city by the British LGBT Awards for successfully welcoming and being popular with the LGBTQ community. Though there is no principal "gay neighborhood" in the city, most gay bars, clubs, hotels, and restaurants are in Palermo. The annual Pride march is in November, attracting over one hundred thousand people.

CHAPTER THREE

CUSTOMS &
FESTIVALS

Folklore occupies a special place in Argentinian culture and is based on the music and customs of the countryside rather than on myths and national stories. The customs and traditions of the early Spanish settlers blended with those of the later European arrivals to give rise to a uniquely Argentinian folk culture. This features the gaucho, traditional forms of clothing such as the poncho, weapons such as *boleadoras*, horse saddles and riding styles, and food and drink. Many of these folk elements have become potent symbols in Argentinian literature, painting, and music, and their importance continues to be upheld, although practices have changed over the years.

There are many days in the calendar that, while not always official public holidays, are celebrated with parades, *asados* (barbecues), pageants, or musical and cultural events. One of the most noteworthy is Día de la Tradición (Tradition Day) on November 10, honoring the birth of nineteenth-century poet José Hernández, the author of the epic *The Gaucho Martín Fierro*.

THE GAUCHO

Gauchos have become one of the legendary symbols of Argentinian culture and tradition, portrayed as the essence of its character in many literary works, perhaps the most renowned being *The Gaucho Martín Fierro,* mentioned above.

The gauchos were nomadic horsemen and cowhands who flourished in the eighteenth and nineteenth centuries in the Argentinian and Uruguayan Pampas, and the south of Brazil. After visiting Argentina and Uruguay in the early 1830s, Charles Darwin shared his observations on the Pampas and its inhabitants: "The Gauchos, or countrymen, are very superior to those who reside in the towns. The Gaucho is invariably most obliging, polite, and hospitable: I did not meet with even one instance of rudeness or inhospitality. He is modest, both respecting himself and country, but at the same time a spirited, bold fellow. On the other hand, many robberies are committed, and there is much bloodshed: the habit of constantly wearing the knife is the chief cause of the latter."

Gauchos made a living by cleaning and preparing leather for the manufacture of goods. Leather was their main source of income as meat had little commercial value in those days, due to its abundant supply for such a small population, the fact that it could not be kept for long periods, and the lack of any kind of export logistics. Gaucho attire, still worn by modern Argentine cowhands, included a *chiripa* girding the waist, a woolen poncho, and long, accordion-pleated trousers called *bombachas*, which are gathered at the ankles and cover the tops of the rider's leather boots. The gaucho lived in small huts called *ranchos*, and the *boleadoras* and the *facón* (see below) were their weapons.

Gauchos have also gone down in history for the role that they played during the wars for independence. The most well known are those led by Martín Miguel de Güemes, who organized the resistance against the Royalists (forces loyal to Spain) in Salta, employing local gauchos who were trained in guerrilla warfare. Each year on June 17, the anniversary of Güemes' death, thousands of gauchos on horseback gather in Salta in their trademark red and black ponchos to honor him.

Boleadoras

These consist of three balls made of stone, wood, and nowadays metal, covered in leather and each attached to a length of rope. A legacy of the early Indigenous

Boleadoras on an Argentinian farm.

peoples who used weighted thongs as a hunting weapon
(with only one ball until the eighteenth century), these
have become a symbol of gaucho culture.

Two variants of the *boleadoras* can be found.
Originally used as a weapon for combat, they developed
into their current form of two balls of approximately
the same dimension and weight that are flung around
in order to gain momentum, plus a smaller ball which
is held in one's hand until the weapon is thrown. For
hunting purposes, the *boleadoras* consist of only two
spheres and are thrown at the prey's legs, wrapping
themselves around and causing the animal to fall over.
These were mainly used to hunt *ñandú*, a local variety
of the ostrich.

Traditional gaucho belt and *facón*.

The *Facón*

The *facón* is a large dagger used as a weapon as well as a utensil. The word is a derivative of *faca* (old Spanish and Portuguese for "knife"), to which the augmentative suffix "*on*" has been added to convey the meaning of "large." A *facón* is a pointed blade about 12 inches (30 centimeters) in length that slides into a sheath originally made of leather, which was usually clipped or attached to the gaucho's belt. Nowadays they are also sold as ornaments made of silver or steel.

The *Ombú*

The *ombú* is a tree closely associated to the Pampas and the gauchos, who would rest in its shade. Despite

A five-hundred-year-old *ombú* tree.

its huge height of 49 to 66 feet (15 to 20 meters), the *ombú* is categorized as a herb because of its hollow trunk, which can grow up to 15 feet (4.5 meters) in diameter. In 1927 it was voted as the national tree. It is a large evergreen that can be found mainly in the east of the country. Isolated in the middle of the vast countryside, its rich foliage and large trunk provide shelter from rain, sun, and wind. Its leaves are also used for medicinal purposes. It cannot be used for carpentry or industrial purposes or even as firewood due to having a hollow trunk. *Ombúes* can be seen outside the Quinta Los Ombúes in San Isidro and at the Museo José Hernández (Chacra Pueyrredón) in Villa Ballester, both on the outskirts of Buenos Aires. Though both are about half an hour from the center of Buenos Aires, they were farms in colonial times and are well preserved.

Truco

This actually translates literally as "trick." It is a card game mainly played in the region of the River Plate (Buenos Aires and Santa Fe, extending to neighboring Uruguay). Played with a pack of forty "Spanish Cards" (*cartas españolas*) as opposed to standard playing cards, it is a fast-moving team game enhanced by a series of gestures that players use to tell each other the cards they hold without tipping off their opponents. It is normally played by two or three groups of two players, with teams inviting each other to accept certain challenges based on the cards in hand. As these are accepted the players start laying their cards on the table, the winning team

A player's hand during a game of *truco*.

being the one holding the cards with the highest value combined with the highest number of points, awarded according to the challenges accepted or declined. While visitors can master the basic rules of *truco*, learning how to play it goes well beyond this; the art remains a great local skill that outsiders will find very hard to master.

MATE: MORE THAN AN INFUSION

Mate (loosely pronounced "mah-tay") is the traditional Argentinian hot drink. The *mate* drinking custom is widespread in Argentina, and although *mate* is an

A cup of the traditional Argentinian hot drink, *mate*.

acquired taste, it's something all visitors should try at least once. The brew is high in caffeine, so expect a buzz!

The word *mate* refers to both the container and the herb (*Ilex paraguariensis*, known as *yerba mate* to differentiate it) that is actually infused. The preparation may sound simple, but there is a hidden art to making *mate* (*cebar un mate*), and a badly prepared offering could be an insult to the connoisseur. The *yerba mate* is infused in hot (not boiling) water in the container (*mate*) and drunk with a sophisticated straw called a *bombilla*. The *bombilla* is normally made of stainless steel, although cane and silver ones can also be found. *Mate* is taken without sugar in most cases (*mate amargo*).

It can be a very social drink and passing one *mate* around a group can be common among drinkers. When drinking it, care must be taken not to block the *bombilla* with the *yerba mate*.

Yerba mate was one of the many new things the Spanish conquistadores came across upon their arrival, together with potatoes, tomatoes, and wheat. *Mate* had initially been banned by the Jesuits, who claimed that the herbs were the cause of the indolence and lethargy of the locals and thus would bring about their own ruin. It was considered a vice, and those breaking the rule would face excommunication.

Mate is now more than an infusion, it is a symbol of the land, and today *mates* can be purchased both for practical and ornamental use.

Mendoza's annual grape harvest festival, la Fiesta de la Vendimia.

NATIONAL CELEBRATIONS

There are countless feasts, festivals, and traditions across the country representative of the cultural backgrounds of the various Indigenous peoples who inhabited the land for centuries. One example is the Quechua festival of Inti Raymi ("Festival of the Sun"), celebrated every year in the city of Salta on June 20, the day of the winter solstice.

There are religious celebrations and festivities such as the pilgrimage to Luján (see page 82) as well as a series of originally pagan celebrations such as Carnaval in the month of February, the Carnaval del País in the city of Gualeguaychú, Entre Ríos, being the most elaborate. Food and harvest festivals are widespread and vary according to the region and the time of year.

Due to the importance of agriculture, many regional festivals are more important for the rural population than for city dwellers, many of whom may not even be aware of their existence.

Many festivals, in particular wine and food festivals, are the direct result of European influence, as opposed to traditional Amerindian festivals, which consist mainly of harvest celebrations or other religious rituals. The Fiesta de la Vendimia (Grape Harvest Festival) in Mendoza in early March is among the largest of its kind in Argentina.

A typical Argentinian *fiesta gaucha* consists of various events such as rodeos (*doma de potro*), where one can witness horsemanship skills at their best, folk music and dancing, and of course, a lavish Argentinian barbecue. The most well-known *fiesta gaucha* is the Festival Nacional de Doma y Folklore de Jesús María in the province of Córdoba, celebrated in January and well worth a visit.

Christmas and Epiphany

The main Christian holidays are strictly observed, Easter and Christmas in particular. Unlike Anglo-Saxon cultures, Christmas Eve rather than Christmas Day holds greater importance. The traditional family occasion consists of dinner on Christmas Eve, when presents are given, with more observant families attending midnight mass.

Many people celebrate Epiphany (Reyes Magos

or simply Reyes) on January 6. Children receive presents on this day rather than on Christmas Eve, especially if they have left out their shoes and water and grass to feed the camels!

Easter and Holy Week

Easter (Pascua) and Holy Week (Semana Santa) play an important part in the Catholic Argentinian calendar, with masses celebrated across the country.

The period of Lent is known as Cuaresma (that is, a period of forty days), and Palm Sunday is known as Domingo de Ramos. Buenos Aires receives thousands of visitors during the Easter period, many of them attending the main Catholic celebrations in Luján and Buenos Aires Cathedral.

Banners with portraits of people who disappeared during General Jorge Rafael Videla's dictatorship, at the Day of Remembrance for Truth and Justice.

PUBLIC HOLIDAYS

There are twelve fixed public holidays in Argentina and four movable ones. These move to the previous Monday if they fall on a Tuesday or Wednesday, or to the following Monday if they fall on a Thursday or Friday.

New Year's Day January 1

Carnaval Celebrated forty days after Lent

Day of Remembrance for Truth and Justice March 24

Veterans' Day April 2

Good Friday March/April

Labor Day May 1

Anniversary of the First National Government
May 25 (known as "Day of the May Revolution")

Martin M Guemes Day June 17 (movable)

Flag Day June 20

Independence Day July 9

Anniversary of the Death of General José de San Martín
August 17 (movable)

Day for the Respect of Cultural Diversity
October 12 (movable)

National Sovereignty Day November 20 (movable)

Day of the Immaculate Conception December 8

Christmas Day December 25

CHAPTER FOUR

MAKING FRIENDS

FRIENDS AND ACQUAINTANCES

Meeting people, making friends, and socializing are as easy in Argentina as in most Latin cultures.

Socializing is a very important aspect of life, and people will rarely miss an opportunity to go out and meet people. Although in Argentina close friends tend to be few in number, people in general will have many acquaintances. Many long-lasting friendships date back to early school days. People may fall out with each other, but Argentinians tend to take friendship seriously and will be quite forgiving.

Visitors to Argentina are welcomed with open arms and the people you get to know will show their hospitality in every possible way. Invitations home are customary, and you'll be made to feel part of your host's circle of friends and acquaintances.

Argentinians love to entertain, and they prefer to do so in their own homes, or their weekend homes (*quintas*) should they have them. Barbecues, coffee evenings, and having guests over for dinner and parties are all characteristic of Argentinian hospitality.

An invitation to Sunday lunch, in many cases a barbecue, is a great occasion to meet people over a meal that can start at noon and still continue four hours later. Repeated invitations signal acceptance into a circle of friends.

Talking is a great Argentinian pastime, be it at home with family or over a coffee at a café with friends. Conversations can go on for hours revolving around the hot button topics of the day, whether they're to do with politics, sports, current affairs, or people's hobbies. People have few inhibitions when it comes to talking and are very direct when expressing their views. Depending on the topic, however, it's not always a good idea as a visitor to offer your own unless asked, and some topics should be avoided until a certain level of familiarity is established. These include the South Atlantic War, a subject that many people are still sensitive about, and Juan Perón (or his wife Eva); you will soon find that Perón was either venerated or hated. Take care when making comparisons between Argentina and other Latin American countries, particularly Brazil with whom there is something of a rivalry.

GESTURES AND PHYSICAL CONTACT

In Argentina, body language is used a lot; touching, hand gestures, and facial expressions all help to convey the speaker's message and enhance the listener's interpretation. There's a list of the key gestures to be aware of below.

When it comes to proxemics (the rules of personal space), Argentinians tend to stand closer to each other than the northern Anglo-Saxons. In the countryside, the rules vary slightly, with people standing a little further away from each other. Intense eye contact should be avoided as it can be construed as challenging or aggressive. Avoiding eye contact, particularly outside the realm of the larger cities, should not be interpreted as a sign of insincerity; intermittent eye contact is probably the best approach.

When greeting someone, handshaking between men and women as well as among women is customary in a business context. When meeting someone socially, things are more informal—kissing someone of the opposite sex on the cheek once is the norm.

SOME DOS AND DON'TS

- The "thumb and forefinger circle" gesture stands for OK—unlike in neighboring Brazil, where it's vulgar and offensive.
- The "thumbs up" gesture can be used freely as it also stands for OK.
- Brushing your chin with the top of your hand outward means "I don't know."
- Beckoning people to come, particularly if accompanied by a "psst" (as is sometimes done in Brazil), is considered rude—Argentinians will normally extend their arm with their hand palm facing down and make a "scratching" motion with the four fingers to beckon someone over.
- Yawning in public is considered rude and is best avoided.

TIMEKEEPING

Timekeeping is mainly determined by context and in more informal situations is almost irrelevant. Start times for concerts, plays, and similar events are normally observed, although a ten-minute delay is not uncommon.

When it comes to parties, lunches with friends, and similar social events, start times are really only indicative. If you're invited to a party, the last thing you should do is arrive on time—in fact, your punctuality might even be considered rude. If arrangements have been made for you to be picked up, flexibility should be observed; waiting by the door ready to go at the prearranged time could result in a long wait. Being kept waiting is quite normal, and if the person you're due to be meeting arrives late and offers no apology, it shouldn't be taken as a lack of respect or consideration. Your Argentinian friend was likely juggling several things at once.

Early dinners in Argentina are not the norm, particularly when eating out. Most restaurants don't serve dinner before 8:00 p.m. and at popular spots it can be hard to find a table as late as midnight, so call ahead to book a table if you're keen on somewhere in particular.

SOCIAL DRINKING

Social life in Argentina can often revolve around wine, which is drunk at most mealtimes. Despite the frequency, Argentinians drink sensibly and with discernment. Public drunkenness is rare and is frowned upon. It's simply not considered a necessary part of having fun. Less sophisticated drinkers will mix wine with soda, particularly less expensive wine. It's also not unusual for parents to give watered-down wine to their children, particularly at barbecues and Sunday family meals.

The province of Mendoza, on the slopes of the Andean foothills, is the country's center of wine production. The long, sunny days, high altitude, stony soil, and wide temperature ranges provide all the necessary ingredients for the making of high-quality wines. Immigrants from Italy, Spain, and France have left their mark on Argentina's wine industry, leading to the planting of a wide range of grapes in the region of Cuyo, with Lujan de Cuyo being renowned for its full-bodied reds and its own appellation. Toward the northwest of the country, the vineyards of Cafayate in the province of Salta are home to a variety of Torrontes, an excellent aromatic dry white wine.

Chardonnay and Pinot Noir are the result of high-altitude vineyards and are among the finest Argentinian wines. Malbec has been for many years the most popular red grape, having yielded Malbec wines in some cases far superior to their French counterparts. Nevertheless, Malbec has given way to other grapes such as Bonarda, Sirah, and Torrontés. From Cabernet Sauvignon to Zinfandel and Nebbiolo, there is no shortage of choice. Caro

2000 by Domaines Barons de Rothschild and Nicolas Catena is a wine that has made its mark; it has a strong Argentinian identity, heralded by Malbec, blended with Cabernet Sauvignon. The combination has made a rich and refined wine, a harmonious balance between the Argentinian and Bordeaux styles. Other wines which have become favorites in the connoisseurs' world are El Enemigo Torrontés 2021 (Bodega Aleanna), Finca Piedra Infinita Gravascal (Familia Zuccardi) and Luigi Bosca's famous Malbec Cabernet Sauvignon blend. Argentina ranked fourth among the top wine-producing countries in 2023 and is considered one of the fastest-growing exporters of wines.

Alcohol is freely available around the clock in bars, and there are no licensing restrictions of any kind other than on the sale of alcohol to minors. Beer drinking has grown in popularity among younger Argentinians. Overall, Argentinians are very self-conscious when it comes to maintaining their dignity, and overt inebriation is considered very unbecoming.

While many cultures get together "for a drink," in Argentina having a coffee (*tomar un café*) is still the norm. This is an activity that takes place in the many pavement bars and cafés of Argentina, from the exclusive La Biela in the elegant district of Recoleta in Buenos Aires to more modest ones all over the country.

GIFT GIVING

Gifts in Argentina are not always physical items. Sometimes a favor in exchange for another is more appropriate and more welcome than a tangible gift (see page 172).

That said, in social contexts it's impolite to arrive at someone's house empty-handed. Chocolate, flowers, or a bottle of (good) wine are appropriate gifts. Bringing something for the hosts' children is always a nice touch, and it need not be anything expensive. For more celebratory occasions like weddings and christenings, Argentinians tend to be very generous. Wedding lists are the norm, and if invited to one, you should try to give a gift from the registry.

If you're traveling to a foreign country, it's a nice touch to ask your friends or colleagues if there's anything they need from that country, as imported goods are heavily taxed and sometimes hard to obtain.

CLUBS AND SOCIETIES

Clubs, with very few exceptions (such as the very exclusive Jockey Club), are relatively easy to join. There are many clubs and gyms where different sports are played and these provide an excellent means of meeting new people and making friends. Membership fees vary according to location, size, and facilities.

For those less athletically inclined there are literary societies, book clubs, and theater groups that carry out their activities in English. Theater groups such as the Suburban Players, who have been staging plays in English for over sixty years, are good entry points for English speakers to mix with expats and Anglo-Argentines without having to worry about the language barrier. The Argentine-British Community Council and the University Women's Club have a calendar of activities and events that offer good opportunities for volunteering and meeting people.

Musical groups such as choral societies are excellent places to meet people and obtain a taste of Argentina's cultural life too. In all cases, having some Spanish under your belt will serve you well and is highly encouraged. For more on language and communicating, see Chapter 9.

CHAPTER FIVE

DAILY LIFE

STANDARDS OF LIVING

Both quality of life and standards of living have changed markedly in recent decades. For many years Argentina's society differentiated itself from the rest of Latin America by having a predominant middle-class majority, with minorities of very affluent and very poor people. Most people enjoyed, with varying degrees of affluence, a relatively good quality of life, and hunger and abject poverty were almost nonexistent.

The socioeconomic changes sparked by political instability and corruption have affected the quality of life and standard of living of Argentinians across the whole spectrum of society. There are still very wealthy people, and Argentina's middle class continues to spend money but at a slower rate. Prosperity and comfort have given way to poverty, hunger, and soaring unemployment, resulting in an increase in violent crime.

There are more enclosed private neighborhoods (called *countries*), and people have become more security conscious than ever before, even though crime rates and threats to personal safety are not as serious as in other Latin American countries.

The number of people living below the poverty line, 36.5 percent of the population in 2022, has risen sharply as a lingering result of hyperinflation, as well as unsound economic policies and austerity plans. People who cannot afford a roof over their heads tend to live in shantytowns (*villas*), which, once confined to the outskirts of the city, have been spreading across more inner-city areas. They are often numbered, for example, *Villa 1-11-14*, or take on names linked to their context, for example, Villa Nicole (which stands for "*Ni colegios ni colectivos*"—No schools and no buses).

For Richer, for Poorer

The Argentinian middle class likes to live well and to appear to be doing so. Restaurants are always full, nightlife is very busy, and, despite difficult economic circumstances, people continue to dress and look much as they would in more prosperous times. It can be baffling to many visitors that aside from street beggars, picket lines, and political demonstrations, life, particularly in large cities, seems to be business as usual.

Welfare provision has increased dramatically since 2001, when only eight hundred thousand people received help from the government. By 2023, that number had risen to just under 12 million. This was criticized as political manipulation by those who were concerned it would encourage some to rely on state handouts as an alternative to work. Despite the increase in state assistance, the number of people living below the poverty line has reached unprecedented levels.

Despite all this, many Argentinians continue to travel abroad, even in the face of currency exchange restrictions and exorbitant surcharges on payments made abroad using credit cards.

SCHOOLS AND EDUCATION

Argentina has a very high literacy rate, with almost 98 percent able to read and write, and is slightly higher amongst women. There are ten years of compulsory school education starting from the age of five. Free state education is provided across the country and caters for 72 percent of school children. The other 28 percent attend private schools, of which more than half are religious. There is also an extensive network of "bilingual schools," teaching the Argentinian curriculum in Spanish and a foreign curriculum in another language, many of them providing the curricula of the International Baccalaureate or British

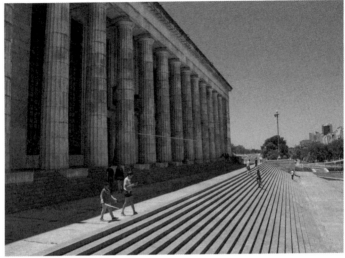

The Faculty of Law at the University of Buenos Aires.

GCSEs and A levels. These schools tend to be expensive and are only afforded by a minority.

The academic year runs from March to November with a break in July (winter holidays) and a long summer break. Some schools have an extra week-long break in the month of September. State school pupils don't wear uniforms but a white pinafore called a *guardapolvo,* which teachers also wear. The Argentinian education system has undergone many changes since the end of the last dictatorship, when the curriculum was biased in terms of content in areas such as history and current affairs, and debate and questioning were not encouraged.

Despite these changes and a move toward a more Socratic approach to education (as opposed, in this case, to autocratic), there is room for improvement and there are still critics of the system who claim that it is inadequate and substandard. As it is, Argentina still produces excellent professionals, scientists, doctors, and artists, including five Nobel laureates, the highest number in Latin America.

When it comes to university education there are private and state universities, and all applicants sit for a common entrance examination (*exámen de ingreso*). Undergraduate education at state universities is free while private establishments charge a fee. University lectures are normally structured in shifts, allowing students to work (even full-time) while studying. Many universities offer late evening timetables from 7:00 to 11:00 p.m. Over the last decade or so, funding for public universities has increased and new universities have been established across the country in densely populated regions not catered for in the past.

NATIONAL SERVICE

Following an incident that led to the death of an eighteen-year-old soldier, which brought to light the way young conscripts were being mistreated in a number of garrisons across the country, compulsory national service (known as *colimba*) was abolished in

1994 during the government of Carlos Menem. This was replaced by voluntary national service whereby volunteers receive remuneration in exchange for their services for up to ten years. There have been talks of a return to a compulsory format for those who neither work nor study, but this remains a controversial issue and no firm decision has been made to date.

HOUSING

The choice of where to live is very much conditioned by the state of the economy, and it's almost impossible

Typical houses in Purmamarca, a village in the province of Jujuy in northwestern Argentina.

The Palermo district in Buenos Aires.

for younger people to buy their own property. The more affluent live in large houses in leafy suburbs or very large apartments in well-kept areas of the city center. In general, Buenos Aires has no shortage of properties to rent, and most young people who move away from home will rent an apartment. These can vary in size and price according to the area in which they're located. In recent years, the offer of rented accommodation has been more limited, however, due to the introduction of legislation which was passed to protect tenants.

Finding a Place to Live

In the main cities finding accommodation is relatively easy, be it apartments to rent or residence inns for shorter stays. There are many real estate agents, and visitors are advised to deal with them through an interpreter or find an English-speaking agent who will look into details such as rates, expenses, and any unresolved legal matters, and contact the building's managing agents. It's always better to sign rental contracts in the local currency with a clause adjusting the price by a fixed percentage, rather than in American dollars, which can suffer astounding fluctuations.

The city center is, as in most countries, where most people live. However, there are options in the suburbs of Argentina's largest cities that are worth considering. Harold Hyland, Reynolds, and Manson are some of the real estate agencies that employ English-speaking staff. Relocation agencies, such as Labs Relocations Services, operate in both English and Spanish. Zonaprop is the most widely used website for finding long-term rentals.

TOWN AND COUNTRY

Argentina is a predominantly agricultural country, and the symbiosis between town and country is perpetuated through the established families of landowners who still earn much of their income from the land but live prosperously in the city. This interdependence becomes evident in events such as the Exposición Rural, which takes place annually in July/August in Buenos Aires. This great exhibition, which has been going on annually for well over a century, offers buyers, breeders, producers, and the general public the opportunity to see Argentina's best livestock and cattle under one roof, from show jumping to cattle shows and prizes for "best of breed" animals. There are also stands promoting the latest agricultural machinery, new hybrid crops, cattle food, and the most recent developments in nutrition and veterinary research. Expoagro, held in the town of San Nicolás in March, is the most important open-air agroindustrial exhibition in Argentina.

DAILY ROUTINE

Daily life in Argentina can be hectic—particularly in Buenos Aires, where people work long hours. In many households where both parents work, children are often looked after by relatives until one of the parents returns home. Shopping, looking after the children, and running a house are carefully balanced to ensure that the children are given the required attention.

USUAL WORKING HOURS AND OPENING TIMES

Banks and Bureaux de Change Monday to Friday
10:00 a.m. to 3:00 p.m.

Office Hours Monday to Friday
9:00 a.m. to 7:00 p.m., lunch break about an hour
between 12:00 p.m. and 2:00 p.m.

Post Offices Monday to Friday
8:00 a.m. to 6:00 p.m., some open on
Saturday 8:00 a.m. to 1:00 p.m.

Shops Monday to Friday
9:00 a.m. to 8:00 p.m., Saturday 9:30 a.m. to 1:00 p.m.

Shopping Centers Monday to Sunday
10:00 a.m. to 10:00 p.m.

The Working Week

Office hours in Argentina are perhaps slightly longer
than elsewhere—from 9:00 a.m. to 6:00 p.m., Monday
to Friday. In the main cities shops are normally open
Monday to Friday from 9:00 a.m. to 8:00 p.m., and
on Saturdays from 9:00 a.m. to 1:00 p.m. Shopping
centers are generally open seven days a week from
10:00 a.m. to 9:00 p.m. (and in some cases as late
as 11:00 p.m.).

The Siesta

Although still a regular habit in provincial towns and
rural communities, the rest period after lunch known
as the siesta is no longer common in Buenos Aires and
other large cities. Perhaps a lingering vestige of the siesta

continues to be the extended lunch break, although fast food and sandwiches seem to have become as prevalent as big sit-down meals, perhaps driven by a combination of a younger generation and budgetary constraints. In the interior of the country, the siesta is a practice still observed, particularly in areas where temperatures can be too high for outdoor work at midday, which in practical terms means that in some towns shops are closed between 1:00 p.m. and 5:00 p.m.

THE COST OF LIVING

With an annual inflation rate of 94.8 percent in 2022, for the majority of the population who earn in pesos, life is a struggle. Increasing inflation is the main worry for Argentinians who have become very price-conscious and more parsimonious in their spending habits. They buy what is strictly necessary and are not loyal to brands or retail chains, but are happy to visit several shops looking for the best prices. In spite of the growth of online shopping, particularly during the pandemic, shopping in person is still the preferred option. The upper middle class still earn relatively good salaries; they keep the restaurants full and continue to vacation abroad. However, when looking at a menu, regardless of class, Argentinians will always keep a close eye on the price column.

For foreign visitors, Argentina is not as inexpensive

as it used to be. This is symptomatic of the current economic instability, inflation, and government policies. Many prices are set at US dollar values and are therefore on a par with international prices. It's possible to find a range of prices to suit different budgets, however.

It is perplexing that one of the richest countries in the world, the breadbasket of Europe during the Second World War, could, as a result of mismanagement and corruption, reach a state of such economic instability.

FAMILY OCCASIONS

There are important milestones in Argentinian family life. Some of these are in line with Catholic tradition. Baptism, First Communion, and weddings are perhaps the three most important events in Argentinian religious life.

Baptisms have changed over the last few years, having become a generally more intimate occasion celebrated in the company of immediate family and perhaps a few friends, although this does vary from family to family. Presents are given and usually consist of silverware, picture frames, books, Christian images, or earrings for girls (normally gold or pearl). Earrings are, probably, the first present baby girls receive, and their ears are pierced only a few days after their birth, often before leaving the hospital. The custom is so ingrained that babies not wearing earrings might be mistaken for a boy!

First Communion can be preceded by several months of religious education (catechism). The church ceremony is followed by a luncheon attended by close family and friends, although nowadays there is a tendency for those who can afford it to mark the occasion with a big celebration. Girls normally wear a white dress and boys wear what is probably their first suit.

Weddings are perhaps the biggest event; ceremonies in the church are normally followed by receptions, ranging from small family gatherings to lavish banquets

A father walks his daughter down the aisle at her wedding ceremony.

and huge parties. The bride will wear a white dress and the groom a suit or other formal attire. By and large, Argentinian weddings are no different from those in many European countries. Registry ceremonies take place a few days before the church wedding.

Secular Celebrations

A girl's fifteenth birthday is a very important event that is traditionally celebrated with a big party (Fiesta de Quince), either at home or in a hotel or similar venue. The girl will usually wear a dress purchased or made specially for the occasion. Traditionally she will have the first dance (usually a waltz) with her father, who will then invite his daughter's partner and the rest of the guests to the dance floor. Nowadays new ideas are often introduced, and the arrangements and entertainments at one event may differ from those at another.

The traditional cake ceremony is worth a mention. The white-frosted cake is attractively decorated with ribbons, and just before it is cut, the young girls present gather round, each taking hold of a ribbon. All together, they pull their ribbons from the cake, and each finds a small charm attached to the end of her ribbon, usually of silver. One of these will be a horseshoe or a ring, to bring good fortune to the lucky recipient.

As with many traditions, things are changing with the times. These days girls often want something different, and perhaps expect more excitement than is offered by an old-fashioned party with cakes, ribbons, and waltzing with their father and uncles. Today, travel agencies offer special packages for fifteen-year-old girls, and those who choose a trip lasting fifteen days, abroad or within the country, seems to be growing in number.

Graduation from school is sometimes celebrated with a class excursion. The destination will vary according to the families' means, with the city of Bariloche in Patagonia remaining a favorite.

CHAPTER SIX

TIME OUT

Argentinians know how to have a good time. Their idea of leisure can vary from a lazy afternoon to a day of sporting activities. Barbecues and entertaining at home are popular; the weather often inspires outdoor leisure activities and men and women tend to spend quite a bit of their leisure time in the sun.

From football matches in public parks to water sports and yachting for the more affluent, Buenos Aires and the center of the country with its more temperate climate provide the ideal conditions for outdoor activities almost all year round.

RESTAURANTS AND COFFEEHOUSES

The café culture that can be seen in cities like Paris or Madrid is very present in Argentinian everyday life. It is still customary for people to get together for

Cafe Tortoni in Buenos Aires, which first opened in 1858.

a coffee in one of the many *confiterías* (tea houses, loosely translated) that can be found in most large cities (see Social Drinking, page 89–91).

When it comes to restaurants, Argentinians are spoiled for choice. Going out for a meal is still very much a social event where conversation can continue over coffee long after the meal is over, the act of which is known as *la sobremesa*.

Food and Drink

Argentina is renowned for its excellent quality of food, catering to everyone from the gourmet to the more functional eater. Compared to many Latin American cuisines, Argentinian food is not normally spicy, and is perhaps not as exotic.

The most typical Argentinian food, and perhaps the one that has gained the best reputation, is beef. *Parrillada* (mixed grill) or *asado,* consisting of barbecued steak as well as various other parts of the animal such as sweetbread, kidneys, and black pudding, are central to Argentinian gastronomic culture. *Chorizo,* a mildly spicy sausage barbecued and served hot, is still the most common appetizer served at barbecues, not to be confused with the Spanish *chorizo,* which is served cold and is more akin to salami. *Choripan, chorizo* between two slices of fresh bread, is a favorite. A generous spoonful of *chimichurri,* a blend of finely chopped parsley, oregano, ground chili, and minced garlic mixed with vinegar and vegetable oil, is often used both on barbecued steak and in a *choripan.* *Empanadas* are small pastries usually filled with meat, chicken, or sweet corn (*humita*); these are served as a first course or appetizer.

The Argentinian hot dog, *choripan.*

Traditional *empanada* pastries.

The influence of the great waves of immigration from Spain and Italy, mainly the latter, can be seen in some aspects of Argentinian cuisine. Argentinian pizza, served with a thicker crust and huge amounts of cheese, has retained its traditional recipe throughout the decades. When it comes to toppings, *muzza*, a pizza with tomatoes, mozzarella cheese, and olives, is probably the most popular variation. Unlike Italy, a large pizza is usually served and shared amongst several people. Italian pasta is served at most restaurants and is always a good back-up option for vegetarians in a country where cuisine is so heavily dependent on meat.

International cuisine has also made its mark in Argentina. French, Japanese, Chinese, Thai, Basque, Greek, Hungarian, and Arab restaurants can be found alongside outlets selling other Latin American cuisines, often from Mexico, Peru, and Chile. Fast-food chains are ubiquitous and can be found in main shopping centers and busier districts.

For Those With a Sweet Tooth

Whether in the afternoon or in the morning, *facturas* are a must. These are delicious pastries that come in various shapes with different fillings such as custard, cream, and jam. *Medialunas* (croissants, literally translated as "half moons") are perhaps the most common form of *facturas*, usually accompanied by a cup of coffee, tea, or hot chocolate. It's interesting to note that *factura* is also the Spanish for "invoice"!

For those wishing to delve into truly Argentinian desserts, *dulce de leche* is a good place to start. Literally translated as "milk jam," it's akin to toffee but softer and lighter. Made from milk and sugar boiled until it acquires a brown color and toffeelike consistency, it's used as a spread or as a filler for pastries and pancakes. Crème caramel (*flan*) topped with a dollop of *dulce de leche* is a popular choice.

Dulce de leche-filled *alfajores*.

A local alternative to the ubiquitous Mars bar, KitKat, or the like is the *alfajor*. This is a small round cake usually covered in chocolate and filled with *dulce de leche*. There are dozens of producers, Havanna and Cachafaz being among the best that can be commonly found.

TIPPING

Tipping is more common in Buenos Aires than elsewhere, although the practice is becoming more prevalent across the country. In restaurants it's customary to leave a tip of 10 percent of the total bill. Some restaurants will include a service charge of up to 25 percent, in which case a minimum tip should suffice.

It is also normal practice to tip hairdressers, ushers in cinemas and theaters, and taxi drivers, the latter usually by rounding up the fare. Otherwise, tips are not generally expected, so you are unlikely to be confronted should you fail to leave one.

Smoking

Smoking is not considered as antisocial a habit as it has come to be regarded in Western Europe or the States; however, anti-smoking awareness campaigns have stepped up their efforts and smoking is no longer allowed in restaurants and bars and, more generally, in closed spaces, including shops, cinemas, theaters, public transportation, and public offices. The ubiquitous "*prohibido fumar*" notice is a visible sign of the times. Despite the usual health warnings, over 20 percent of the adult population still partake in the habit.

ARGENTINIAN TABLE MANNERS

- Don't blow your nose at the table.
- Use cutlery in the same way as you would in continental Europe—fork in the left hand with tines facing down and knife in the right hand—but avoid using toothpicks (although there will probably be some on most restaurant tables).
- Keep both hands on the table; try to avoid eating with one hand on your lap.
- When finishing your meal, place your knife and fork together on the plate.
- As in most Spanish-speaking countries, the word used for a toast is *Salud!* (literally, "health"). You can also say this to someone who has just sneezed, or would like to sneeze at some point in the future but can't at present.

Crowds at the traditional San Telmo Market in Buenos Aires.

SHOPPING

Shopping in Argentina, especially in Buenos Aires, can be quite an experience. Stylish and fashionable shops abound, with many local designers alongside the renowned international labels.

Clothes, footwear, leather goods, books, and antiques are only some of the things that are on offer across a huge number of retail outlets. There are many shopping centers across Buenos Aires, most of them offering a plethora of outlets to meet all budgets, from the stylish Patio Bullrich in the city center to large American-style shopping malls in the suburbs with shops, food outlets, and cinemas. These are also convenient as they have longer opening hours than usual, normally from 10:00 a.m. to 10:00 p.m., including Sundays.

Buenos Aires has many shopping districts, from the stylish, elegant, and quite pricey Recoleta to more modestly priced retailers like those found on Avenida Santa Fe. Florida, a pedestrian street since 1913, is still an important retail area stretching over 1,094 yards (1 kilometer) from the elegant San Martín Square (Plaza San Martín) to Avenida de Mayo, where a variety of shops, cafés, and arcades can be found. It is still a shopping landmark of the city center of Buenos Aires.

Round-the-clock shopping is not usual; where available, usually in shopping centers, it's restricted to the main cities and to certain dates such as a few days before Christmas. In smaller cities and provincial towns, lunch breaks can be quite long and, as previously mentioned, it's not uncommon to find shops closed between 1:00 p.m. and 4:00 or 5:00 p.m. Sunday trading is also limited to larger cities, with varying opening times. Gas stations usually open early in the morning and close at midnight.

Though digital payment methods experienced a surge in use over the course of the Covid-19 pandemic, cash is still widely used, even more so because many shops offer a 10 percent discount for cash payments. The most widely used credit card in

Argentina is Visa. If your credit or debit card is issued abroad, the official exchange rate will be used.

The principal platform for online shopping for both new and second-hand products in Argentina is the ever-popular Mercado Libre, while Pedidos Ya and Rappi are used for deliveries. For more on handy apps worth downloading, see page 195.

Kioskos

Kioskos are very much part of the character of Argentina's towns and cities. Like newsagents in the UK, *kioskos* normally sell confectionery, cigarettes, and soft drinks. These are usually small shops, some no more than a counter or shop window, with the customer being served on the sidewalk. Normally found in stations and busy streets or near bus stops, the *kioskero* will always readily help in giving directions or local travel information. The more centrally located *kioskos* are often open 24/7.

Duty-Free Shopping

In line with most taxes in Argentina, value-added tax (VAT) is quite high at 21 percent. If buying goods in Argentina, one can reclaim the VAT (IVA, *impuesto al valor agregado*) on items over a certain value ($70 or

US $1 at the time of writing). It's important to point out that only single transactions of a product made in Argentina of this value or over will qualify for a VAT refund.

VAT can be reclaimed on purchases made in outlets that are registered with the VAT office. These display the traditional "tax free" logo in the window. It's worth asking before purchasing, particularly if the purchase in question is of high value, as the tax refund can be quite considerable.

If you need to get a VAT refund, you should allow plenty of time when going to the airport. You'll need to get the relevant forms from the retailer and once you've gone through the formalities at customs, you'll be paid the refund in cash, a debit to your credit card, or a personal check.

MONEY MATTERS

Argentina's national currency is the Argentine peso. Note that it has the same symbol ($) as the American dollar. This means that prices expressed using the $ symbol are in Argentine pesos and those expressed in American dollars use the symbol: US$.

Banks and cash machines (*cajeros automáticos*) are found in most places in main cities. Care should be taken when withdrawing cash from machines on account of an increase in muggings. At the time of writing there are restrictions on the amount and number of withdrawals that a tourist can make at a cash machine and commissions are high. There are various retail banks, many of them branches of international main street banks such as HSBC, Citibank, and BNP Paribas.

There are also many currency exchange offices (*casas de cambio*). It's best to check the rate of exchange and the amount of commission payable first. US dollars are easier to exchange than pounds sterling, although euros are also accepted by most banks and *bureaux de change*. Like in many other countries there is a parallel (or *blue*) market offering a much more favorable exchange rate for foreign currencies, particularly the US dollar (known as *el dólar blue* to distinguish this from the official exchange rate). Changing money in the street from *arbolitos* (literally, "little trees," men who change "greens," i.e. dollars) will provide a better exchange rate (almost twice the official rate). However, this is against the law and can pose a risk to personal safety and result in potential prosecution.

THEATER AND CINEMA

The Argentinians are great theater and cinema lovers. Movie buffs will find that Argentina has more to offer when it comes to choice of films than many

The inside of Teatro Colón, a renowned performance venue in Buenos Aires.

other places in Latin America. Blockbuster American films are shown alongside French and Spanish films, productions from other countries, and, of course, Argentinian films, many of which have won the acclaim of international audiences and critics. Films in Argentina are subtitled and not dubbed except on very rare occasions.

Buenos Aires boasts over sixty cinemas and three hundred and fifty theaters, which makes it the city with the most vibrant theatrical scene in Latin America. Although productions are in Spanish, there are a few amateur and semiprofessional groups that stage productions in English, notably composed of members of the Argentinian-British community. Groups such as the Suburban Players have been staging high-quality plays and musicals for decades. They offer a way for visitors to get involved with the local community without the language barrier, by either acting or performing more administrative tasks. Timbre 4, an independent theater, occasionally offers plays subtitled in English.

The cultural centers of Borges, Recoleta, Kirchner, General San Martín, and Usina del Arte are hubs of national and international cultural activities, featuring concerts, recitals, plays, exhibitions, and lectures.

NIGHTLIFE

There is no shortage of nightlife in Argentina's main cities and holiday resorts during peak periods. Bars and restaurants are open until the early hours of the morning, and finding a table in a popular restaurant even as late as midnight can be a problem.

Buenos Aires nightlife is probably among the most active in the world. The more affluent Porteños will kick off the evening with a meal, which will rarely start before 10:00 p.m. Clubs and discos open fashionably late—there's not much point in arriving earlier than 1:00 a.m.

Fashion consciousness is at its peak in some of the most exclusive bars in Buenos Aires, where dress is smart yet informal. Palermo, Las Cañitas, Puerto Madero, and Recoleta are at the center of nightlife, with many bars, restaurants, and clubs accounting for busy streets all night long. Tango bars and shows, jazz cafés, and live music venues are mainly found in the city center, with many bars serving food too. Cinemas have late night performances and many theaters offer two evening performances on weekends.

Argentina (and Buenos Aires in particular) is still a favorite destination of many international bands and musicians. Venues for larger events include football stadiums (River Plate being one of the largest and most popular) and the Luna Park, an indoor arena in the city center of Buenos Aires.

LOTTERY AND GAMBLING

Gambling laws have been relaxed since the arrival of the democratic process in Argentina. Casinos now operate in most provinces, offering the usual range of games such as blackjack, roulette, baccarat, and slot machines. The casino in Buenos Aires is located in the busy nightlife district of Puerto Madero on a Mississippi-style boat. Casinos can also be found in most popular seaside resorts, such as Mar del Plata and Pinamar.

The lottery (Lotería Nacional) has a series of gambling products such as La Grande, the largest lottery prize draw in Argentina, which has been in existence since the late nineteenth century. Bingo, *quiniela* (a type of lottery), and lotto are also available. El Gordo de Navidad is the big lottery draw at Christmastime. The draw is broadcast on the radio, and the winning numbers are "sung" by children as they are drawn. This Christmas draw has been taking place for over a century, with the top prize reaching 86 million pesos (about US $470,000 in 2023).

Football pools in Argentina are called PRODE, an abbreviation of *pronosticós deportivos* (literally translated as "sports forecast"). There are thirteen matches, whose results must be correctly guessed in order to win. Prizes are awarded for thirteen, twelve, or eleven correct results for football matches played on Saturdays or Sundays.

Horse racing is very popular, representing the fourth-most popular form of gambling after casinos, *quiniela*, and bingo.

SUMMER PLACES

The choice of summer resorts varies according to taste and budget. The seaside resorts of the Atlantic coast are by far the most popular as they are within easy reach of the main cities of Buenos Aires, Córdoba, and Rosario, and there is plenty of accommodation at various price points. Places like Mar del Plata and

Popular summer getaway destination San Carlos de Bariloche.

Pinamar (about 250 miles from Buenos Aires) attract many visitors during January and February.

The hills of Córdoba are also a popular destination for those who seek a vacation away from the crowds as they offer hiking, cycling, and fishing. There are plenty of hostels and hotels in the area, as well as a wide range of properties to rent.

The landscapes and natural beauty of the winter ski resorts in the south of the country attract visitors from all over the world in summer too. Lakes, mountains, and the great outdoors are the choice of many families, both with and without children, as it is in these areas where summers are not as hot as in the rest of the country.

One of the most exclusive summer resorts continues to be the seaside resort of Punta del Este across the River Plate in neighboring Uruguay. This is where the affluent Argentinians spend their summer vacation along with visitors from many other countries; even the former Shah of Iran used to have a house there. The resort thrives on tourism, with beaches, all-night clubs, restaurants, yachting, and properties on a par with many Beverly Hills mansions. For the younger generation, Punta del Este is the place to be seen, and although many people consider it a "poser's paradise" akin to many Californian resorts, it's still the chosen destination for many well-to-do Argentinians.

Some people own a holiday home in Argentina, often in the south or in the most popular seaside resorts. Those who own farms or *estancias* will opt to spend all or part of their vacation there.

Open Spaces

Whether in a small rural town or a large city, squares (*plazas*) are always found. Large cities tend to have many squares and green spaces. Palermo is a vast area of Buenos Aires with several parks, surrounded by an elegant residential area. There are many attractions in these gardens, including the planetarium, a boating lake, the botanical gardens, and the zoological gardens, which have recently reopened as an eco-park. Palermo also has smaller enclosed gardens such as a Japanese-style garden, a rose garden, and a patio built in Andalusian style. Other main cities have no shortage of green spaces, such as Parque Sarmiento in Córdoba and Parque San Martín in Mendoza, which also houses the zoo.

The trees in Buenos Aires offer a free, natural spectacle throughout the year. In autumn the *palo borracho* (white floss-silk tree) is in bloom in Plaza San Martin and along the 9 de Julio Avenue. The pink flowers of the huge *lapacho* (pink trumpet tree) on the corner of Ramón Castillo and Figueroa Alcorta mark the beginning of spring. In November, the purple flowers of the jacarandas give the city a unique look and the massive *tipas* (rosewood trees) on both sides of the streets offer comforting protection from the sun in summer.

HIGH CULTURE

The European roots of Argentinian society are reflected in much of its music, literature, and lifestyle. Concerts, recitals, and ballet, although only found in main cities, are of very high quality. No visitor should leave Buenos Aires without visiting the magnificent Opera House (Teatro Colón), one of the best of its kind in the world and with acoustics that are second to none. Its sumptuous auditorium, which has been host to the world's top orchestras and

Tigre Art Museum (Museo de Arte de Tigre) in Buenos Aires Province.

artists for almost a century, also houses the Buenos Aires Philharmonic Orchestra. The Teatro Colón offers guided tours lasting about an hour, some of them in English. Please note children in pushchairs are not allowed to join these tours.

The Italian and German influence in Argentina laid the foundation for a great operatic tradition. The opera season at the Teatro Colón features many of the works in the standard repertoire alongside lesser-known pieces. The theater has become a source of Argentinian pride and a point of reference for performers and musicians all around the world for its opera and music performances.

For those interested in music and singing, there are many choral societies that visitors can join. These will provide the enthusiast with the chance to get involved in local cultural life and to sing under the baton of some of the world's great conductors.

Argentinian visual arts and literature also offer an interesting combination of European cultural heritage and local culture. In Buenos Aires, The National Fine Arts Museum (Museo Nacional de Bellas Artes), Museum of Modern Art (Museo de Arte Moderno), Museum of Hispano-American Art (Museo de Arte Hispanoamericano), MALBA (Buenos Aires Museum for Latin American Arts), and Museum of Decorative Arts (Museo de Arte Decorativo), have a varied program of exhibitions and lectures, many of them free. Museums are open five days a week, normally Tuesday to Saturday and in some cases Wednesday to Sunday; it is advisable to check before going. Most museums are closed on Mondays.

An Underground Art Center?

The Teatro Colón was originally located in Plaza de Mayo on the land now occupied by the Banco de la Nación Argentina. The need for a larger auditorium prompted the construction of the current building, inaugurated in 1908. In 2001 it was closed temporarily for extensive restoration works, reopening in 2010. It occupies about 86,000 square feet (8,000 sq. m), of which 54,000 square feet (5,000 sq. m) belong to the building itself, while an astonishing 32,000 square feet (3,000 sq. m) lie below Arturo Toscanini Street, housing all the workshops, wardrobes, rehearsal halls, and catering facilities, and the music, ballet, singing, and experimental academy (Instituto Superior de Arte del Teatro Colón).

Argentina has produced many celebrated artists across many disciplines: Jorge Luis Borges, Ernesto Sábato, and Julio Cortázar in literature; Raul Soldi, Quinquela Martín, and Antonio Berni in painting; and Martha Argerich, Daniel Barenboim, and Lalo Schifrin in music.

Buenos Aires has more bookshops per inhabitant than any other city in the world, including Librería de Avila, founded in 1785, to the impressive Ateneo Grand Splendid, housed in what used to be a theater and was voted the second most beautiful bookshop in the world by National Geographic in 2019. Despite the cultural centralization of Buenos Aires, where most museums and art galleries are also found and where most cultural events take place, archaeology, natural sciences, and natural history museums can be found in other cities, too.

POPULAR CULTURE

Tango

It would be difficult and unfair to ascribe a single popular culture to Argentina—you'll encounter many as you travel across the country. Many areas have their own music and traditions. Perhaps the most widespread is the popular Porteño culture, in view of the fact that 33 percent of the population live in the city of Buenos Aires and its suburbs.

Tango is perhaps one of the most famous popular music styles in the world. It is not, however, a national dance. It's found mainly in Buenos Aires, with other parts of the country having their own dance forms. Tango originated as a dance among the impoverished classes of Buenos Aires, characteristic of *bordellos* (brothels) and bars. It eventually developed into music that captivated the whole of society even as it maintained the underlying tones of melancholia and desperation that characterize the genre. The arrival on the scene of great exponents like Carlos Gardel transformed the perception of tango and earned it a coveted place in the popular culture of the city. Tango is a genre that can be found in purely instrumental or sung forms. Lyrics reflect the sadness and joy of Porteño life and its characters, and are marked by melancholy and sorrow.

Tango continues to flourish as a musical style and has transcended the boundaries of Buenos Aires' popular culture through the work of artists such as Astor Piazzolla. There has been a rise in the popularity of tango among the younger generation over the last couple of decades. Many schools have their own dedicated tango dance groups and even their own tango orchestras. There has been a large increase in the number of places where you can learn how to dance tango; this is an excellent way of taking in the local culture, as are the many venues where tango is performed.

The district of La Boca in Buenos Aires remains the place that embodies the spirit of tango. Certain parts can be rather touristy, but it still retains a character that makes it worth spending a few hours in.

Folk Music
There are several styles within Argentinian folk music, a genre perhaps musically not as sophisticated as tango,

which developed much under European influence.
It is in the folk traditions that the influence of the
Indigenous peoples who inhabited Argentina at the
time of colonization becomes palpable.

There are several musical forms, including
baguala, which originated among cultures such as the
Diaguitas and Calchaquíes. These forms originated
in Salta and spread to the high plains of the Andes.
This is music still strongly built upon a five-note
(pentatonic) scale that can vary from slow and gentle
to quite vivacious in the high plains of Salta and Jujuy.
Yaraví originated in the Inca culture of Peru and
made its way to the northern part of Argentina. It
expresses pain and sorrow.

These old musical forms have given way to today's
musical styles, such as *zamba*, *gato*, *chacarera*, and
chamamé. Most of these are played on a guitar
accompanied by percussion (normally a drum, or
bombo), and in the case of *chamamé*, indigenous to
the area of Mesopotamia, an accordion also features.

Carnavalito is a style very characteristic of the
region of the Puna up in the Andes that shares
a lot in character with the music of Bolivia and
Peru. Typical of this genre is the use of many
regional instruments, such as the *quena* (similar
to a recorder), the *siku* (also known as the "pan
flute"), and the *charango*, a stringed instrument
whose sound box is made from the carcass of an
armadillo (*mulita*) with a wooden lid covering it

and a fingerboard attached. Originally fitted with gut strings, modern versions are made of wood and fitted with metal or nylon strings. The style of *carnavalito* and its typical instruments was used by Simon and Garfunkel in their 1970 hit "If I Could" (also known as "El Condor Pasa").

SPORTS

There is no shortage of sporting activities in Argentina, and facilities for most of them are quite good. A wide range of sports is played, with football being the most popular. The infrastructure for professional football is very good, with some stadiums seating over forty thousand people. Although the last World Cup held here was over forty years ago, the stadiums built for the event are still in very good shape. In 1978, despite controversy about the politics of the military government, Argentina hosted the football World Cup, with Buenos Aires as the focal point for the event. This had a deep impact on the infrastructure of the city and its attitude to visitors. Argentina's victory helped unite the country and briefly created an atmosphere of joy and celebration. Argentinians are still passionate about the sport—all the more so after their sweeping victory at the 2022 World Cup tournament. At home, the rivalry between the two main teams, River Plate and Boca Juniors, continues to dominate the football scene in Buenos Aires and, indeed, across most of the country. For the football enthusiast, the traditional River Plate versus Boca Juniors match is perhaps the single most important football game in the first division.

The British influence again makes its mark when it comes to rugby, tennis, polo, and golf. Los Pumas, Argentina's national rugby team, are almost always present at international rugby tournaments. Since 2012 Los Pumas have played in the Rugby Championship with Australia, New Zealand, and South Africa and have been the South American champions since 2009. There are several rugby clubs you can join that offer opportunities to players of most ages and abilities. The Buenos Aires Lawn Tennis Club hosts international tournaments featuring many of the world's top-seeded players and offers well-structured courses and coaching. Again, there are several clubs you can join, many of them dedicated tennis clubs.

Polo is a sport dominated by the more affluent sectors of society. Argentinian polo is renowned for the high standard of its players and the best of breed horses used. Many international figures, including King Charles, have at one time or another played polo in Argentina. *Pato* is the popular form of polo; it was declared the national sport in 1953. It is played on horseback, and the ball (the *pato*) is caged inside leather straps with handles so that the players can

Players of *pato*, a popularized version of polo.

seize it and pass it to each other. The object of the game is to score points by putting the *pato* through a metal hoop. It is a fast-paced sport that requires a fair amount of bravado.

Along Argentina's coast, particularly in the province of Buenos Aires, a large number of enthusiasts take to the water in their crafts. Sailing, waterskiing, rafting, and motorboating can be practiced all year round. There are several yacht clubs within easy reach of the city center, and particularly the suburbs to the north of the center, offering excellent and convenient mooring facilities.

The resorts in the south of the country offer the opportunity to practice winter sports in well-equipped centers with very good infrastructure for skiing and snowboarding. For the more adventurous and experienced enthusiast, mountain climbing in the Andes offers challenges equal to many of the world's large mountain ranges. Hang gliding and rafting have been gaining popularity over the years, aided by the country's spectacular scenery and geography.

Argentina's climate is ideal for golfing. Fertile land and a temperate climate provide the conditions for excellent turf and all-year-round playing. Golf came to Argentina with the British in 1879 when a Scotsman, Henry Smith, arrived with the first set of golf clubs. The Argentinian Golf Association organizes national and international tournaments.

The Golfing Craze

There are more golf links in Argentina than in the rest of Latin America combined. The Argentinian Golf Association lists nearly three hundred affiliated courses, including several par three courses, and administers the handicap of almost forty-five thousand players nationwide!

CHAPTER SEVEN

TRAVEL, HEALTH, & SAFETY

WHEN TO GO

It's worth remembering that the seasons in the southern hemisphere are the opposite of those in the northern hemisphere. The high season in Argentina is January and February, when schools break for the summer vacation. There are also winter school vacations in July. As Argentinians escape to their favorite resorts by the seaside in the south of the country or in the hills of Córdoba, accommodation and transportation can be harder to find and is usually more expensive. Advance booking is recommended during these busy periods.

Buenos Aires can be visited all year round. December, January, and February can be very hot and humid, though there is a special beauty to the quieter city during these months. Days are long during the summer, making this the ideal time of year to visit

Friends enjoy the temperate summer climate at Lago Escondido in Patagonia.

Patagonia, where temperatures are more bearable than during the cold and blustery winters. Conversely, the soaring temperatures in the north and northwest means this region is not the best summer destination. During winter (June to August) temperatures are more bearable, although they can drop sharply after sunset. For those seeking to admire the subtropical vegetation and natural beauty of the Iguazú Falls, one of the sites outside Buenos Aires which should not be missed, winter and spring are the best times to visit as the weather is cooler and there is less rain.

The winter months offer the ski enthusiast the opportunity to take to the slopes in one of the many resorts in the Andean region of the country. Needless to say, adequate clothing is required for the sub-zero temperatures.

ENTERING ARGENTINA

A valid passport is required to enter Argentina and should be valid for the proposed duration of your stay. No additional period of validity beyond this is required. Nationals of some countries will also require a visa; check online. Visitors arriving from non-neighboring countries are allowed to bring in up to US $500 in goods without paying any import duty or local taxes and an additional US $500 in goods acquired in local duty-free shops. This is correct at the time of print but visitors are advised to check online before arriving to avoid charges.

Visitors are normally permitted to remain up to ninety days as a tourist. If you envisage a longer stay, it's best to check with the consulate before departure as to what should be done to avoid unnecessary delays and being caught up in the Argentinian bureaucratic apparatus when trying to extend your stay.

Proof of Covid-19 vaccination is not required to enter Argentina. Once in the country, visitors should take the necessary precautions to avoid being bitten by mosquitoes as dengue fever can be transmitted throughout the year. The mosquito that spreads dengue is more common in urban areas. There is a risk of dengue in the provinces of Buenos Aires, Catamarca, Chaco, Cordoba, Corrientes, Entre Rios, Formosa, Jujuy, Misiones, Salta, Santa Fe, Santiago del Estero, and Tucuman.

Argentina possesses a very high standard of inoculation campaigns, and the vast majority of the population is inoculated against polio, smallpox (now eradicated), and tuberculosis. By 2023, over 90 percent of the population had received one dose of the Covid-19 vaccine, while approximately 70 percent had received two doses or more.

Plants, fruits and vegetables, and perishable foods are not allowed into Argentina. Pets are allowed provided adequate proof of vaccination can be shown. This has at times proven complicated, however, so visitors traveling with a pet should ensure they are well informed before departing.

TRAINS

Despite the once great train network that boasted over 24,856 miles (40,000 kilometers) of railways, trains today are only used for suburban to city-center commuting and are no longer commonly used for long-distance journeys. Sadly, this once enviable network became the victim of neglect and lack of investment. Long-distance trains are not very

The Tren a las Nubes (Train to the Clouds) in Salta.

comfortable, serve few destinations, and services are not frequent. Journeys can take many hours, and for those who can afford it, flying has become the preferred means of long-distance travel.

There are four terminal railway stations in Buenos Aires where frequent and reliable services to the suburbs depart and arrive at regular intervals. Train services to the seaside town Mar del Plata and the southern city of Bariloche are perhaps the most popular and are still widely used by travelers during the holiday season. Fares are relatively inexpensive and early booking is recommended, particularly in summer. For those with more time on their hands and a penchant for off-the-beaten-track experiences, the

Tren a las Nubes ("Train to the Clouds"), leaving from Salta, follows a route of breathtaking scenery across the northern Andes, reaching 4,220 meters above sea level. Advance bookings are recommended.

BUSES

Colectivos

Buses, commonly known as *colectivos*, are one of the most popular means of transportation in Argentina. In large cities there are many different lines, with over

A Metrobus at Teatro Colón Station in Buenos Aires.

one hundred and thirty operating in Buenos Aires; they are clearly numbered and easily distinguishable, as most lines have distinctive colors and designs. A prepaid travel card (*tarjeta SUBE*) must be used on buses, trains, and subways. This can be ordered online or purchased at SUBE outlets (enter "SUBE" into Google Maps to find the location of outlets nearby). They can be topped up online and at cashpoints, *kioskos*, lottery shops, SUBE automatic kiosks, and at most railway stations.

Bus drivers are proud of their vehicles and many of them display ornate decorative objects—hanging plastic dice, flashing gearshift knobs, decorated rearview mirrors—and keep their buses very clean. Smoking isn't allowed, and although eating is not explicitly forbidden it's frowned upon; you might be asked to put your lunch away!

Bus stops are located at regular intervals, every two or three blocks. Boarding is normally done via the front door, alighting at the rear. Buses only stop at the request of a passenger so when you're ready to get off the bus, alert the driver using the bell located above the rear door, ideally a block or two before the stop.

A network of dedicated bus lanes known as Metrobus operates in Buenos Aires and in some districts in the suburbs, offering covered bus shelters and travel information. The system operates on selected main avenues. Not all buses operate in these lanes and while the system has helped to ease congestion not all buses follow the Metrobus route its entire length.

Long-Distance Coaches

The long-distance coach service in Argentina is quite good and there is a wide network of routes from Buenos Aires to all the other provinces as well as to neighboring countries, mainly Uruguay, Paraguay, and Brazil. Coaches offer a standard service and a slightly better option (*diferencial*). The former is cheaper—seats are not guaranteed and do not have air-conditioning or heating, which given the extreme temperatures to be found in Argentina is something travelers should bear in mind. The latter option is more expensive but well worth it, particularly for long journeys. It offers comfortable reclining seats and, in some cases, flat beds for long-distance travel, air-conditioning, and heating. Many have an onboard service offering basic snacks and drinks.

Coach services depart from Buenos Aires Bus Terminal (Terminal de Buenos Aires) near Retiro rail station. There are over one hundred coach lines operating from this terminal, and tickets can be purchased at the terminal or online. The website Plataforma 10 sells tickets online for most operators, while some operators have their own websites. Passengers are asked for an identity document to purchase a ticket and will be expected to show it on boarding the coach. As in all locations where there are a large numbers of tourists, passengers using the terminal should pay attention to their personal belongings.

TAXIS

Taxis are common and are an easy and relatively cost-effective way of getting around in Argentina's cities. In Buenos Aires there are over twenty-seven thousand registered taxis, but it's not always necessarily easy to find one! City taxis are black with a yellow roof and display their license number on the doors in yellow letters. They circulate day and night and can be hailed anywhere in the street. The cost of the journey is metered, and tipping is usually done by rounding up the fare. As in many cities, there are a few drivers who might try to take advantage of potentially unsuspecting visitors. Things to be aware of are longer routes, counterfeit notes (especially at night), and switching bank notes for ones of a lower value. Wearing a seat belt is compulsory, but most people in the back seat do not comply with this and you may find that they are often out of order.

Both Uber and Cabify operate in Buenos Aires along with other main cities and have grown considerably in recent years. Helpfully, Cabify also accepts cash payments. The city of Buenos Aires has also developed its own ride-hailing app, BA Taxi, which allows you to order a classic black and yellow taxi. Radio taxis, more popular once than they are today, are ordered by telephone and will collect you at an agreed-upon address. This is a safer alternative to flagging down a cab at night, as are the apps.

Remises

Remises are privately owned vehicles akin to minicabs in the UK. The price of the journey is fixed in advance—this ensures a slightly better service and that the driver will take the most direct route to the passenger's destination. The *remise* is normally slightly more expensive than a taxi—prices are usually verbally agreed upon—and is frequently used for journeys to and from the airport. At most airports in Argentina companies offering these services can easily be spotted in the arrivals area.

The use of *remises* has become a preferred option for many and is probably recommended over a taxi as it is considered safer.

THE METRO

Buenos Aires has an extensive underground network, which is in fact the oldest in Latin America. The metro is referred to as the *subterráneo*, or *subte* for short, and consists of five lines (named A to E, and H) serving ninety stations across its 35 miles (57 kilometers) of network. In the outskirts of Buenos Aires there also is a light railway, called Premetro, that connects with the E line. Although perhaps not the most comfortable way to get around Buenos Aires (it can be noisy and quite hot in summer) it's quick and efficient and is used by 1.36 million commuters daily. The *subte* runs from Monday to Saturday from 6:00 a.m. to 9.00 or 10:00 p.m. (depending on the line), and Sunday from 8:00 a.m. to 10:00 p.m. Tickets are one fixed price and can be purchased at stations. Most people use the *tarjeta SUBE*, the same one used on buses and trains, which can be topped up at stations or online.

Entrance to the underground *subte* station in the Palermo district of Buenos Aires.

BOATS

There is a good ferry service between Argentina and Uruguay. The largest company is Buquebus, offering daily services between Buenos Aires and the cities of Colonia and Montevideo and the Uruguayan seaside resort of Punta del Este. Although relatively costly, this service is fast and efficient, with a modern fleet of boats able to carry both passengers and cars. This option reduces the length of the journey to Uruguay should you decide to go by car. For a good view of Buenos Aires, see the one-hour boat rides that leave from Puerto Madero to the delta in Tigre.

DRIVING

Car rental in Argentina can be expensive, although it does offer a great amount of flexibility. There are a number of car rental companies, including the major international ones (Avis, Hertz, and Europcar) as well as local firms. These can be found in most cities and popular tourist destinations. Visitors can use their country's driver's license, but must be eighteen or over.

Expressways are privately run in Argentina and there are toll booths along the way. They are well maintained and are usually quite wide, particularly near major cities. They tend to become less reliable further away from those cities. There are many gas stations along the

RULES OF THE ROAD

A certain amount of bravado is required to drive in Argentina. Sadly, many basic rules are not followed and it has one of the highest accident rates in the world. Visitors are advised to stay below the speed limit and follow the highway code. Drivers tend to be short-tempered and can be quite aggressive—the horn is constantly used, and bus drivers rule the roads.

- It's compulsory to wear a seat belt, even if locals don't always follow the rules.
- Traffic drives on the right.
- In built-up areas the speed limit is 25 mph (40 kmph) on small roads and 37 mph (60 kmph) on large avenues. On expressways the speed limit is 75 mph (120 kmph), but it is only 50 mph (80 kmph) on main roads.
- Left turns at traffic lights are not allowed unless there is a filter light with an arrow.
- Headlights should be on during the daytime.
- There are hefty penalties for driving under the influence of alcohol.

expressways, but for long journeys, particularly on off-expressway country roads, service stations might be harder to find. In Argentina, gasoline is known as *nafta*.

Country roads tend to be old, poorly maintained, and often badly signposted.

Parking

It is always best to park in a parking lot (*playa de estacionamiento*), which is usually supervised. Street parking is allowed, but drivers are strongly advised to make sure they are legally parked. Tow trucks (*grua*) and clamps (*cepo*) are in operation in main cities.

Driving in Buenos Aires

Despite its broad avenues and synchronized traffic lights, traffic in Buenos Aires can be chaotic, and drivers tend to be more aggressive than in smaller towns and rural areas.

Traffic is disorderly and the driving attitude is very offensive, with little if any respect for other drivers and even less for pedestrians.

Rules of the road are ignored more often than not, particularly red traffic lights late at night, as a result of the rise in robberies. Driving is thus not recommended for less confident drivers.

Driving Abroad

From Argentina, one can easily drive to neighboring

countries. There are expressways that cover long distances to Chile, Bolivia, Paraguay, Brazil, and Uruguay, although the latter is more easily reached by ferry (see page 152), and with a significant reduction in journey length. The ferry is also recommended if you are driving to Brazil. Passports should be left in a hotel safe or security box when not being used.

There are border controls where a passport and visa (if required) should be produced, together with your vehicle registration documents and insurance policy. It's advisable to check with the authorities for the most up-to-date requirements. The Automóvil Club Argentino provides information on most driving-related services, including roadside assistance and insurance.

FLYING

There are fifty-five airports used for passenger flights. The main airport is Ezeiza Airport (EZE), located about 22 miles (34 kilometers) from the city center of Buenos Aires. This is where most international flights arrive and depart to Europe, the USA, and various Latin American destinations. For air travel from Buenos Aires to other provinces, or to Uruguay and some Brazilian destinations, there is a regular and frequent schedule from Aeroparque Jorge Newbery (AEP), located only fifteen minutes from the center of Buenos Aires.

There are more than four hundred flights operating

daily; most routes are operated by Aerolineas Argentinas, the main national airline, although other, smaller airlines offer scheduled services to selected destinations. Two low-cost airlines that operate internal flights are JetSMART and Flybondi. Tickets can be purchased online directly from the airlines or online through Despegar.

For transfers to/from airports, visitors are advised to take only licensed taxis, *remises,* or use Uber or Cabify. It is best to avoid services offered by men standing outside the airport.

London in Argentina

The land upon which Jorge Newbery Airport is built was reclaimed from the River Plate and, according to some, filled with rubble from the bombing of London in the Second World War. The ships that transported grain and cereals from Argentina to Europe during the war had to carry some ballast on their way back. It was this ballast that was used to fill the reclaimed land.

CYCLING

There are ample opportunities for cycling around the country. Mountain biking has become increasingly popular and many enthusiasts visit the south of the

Cyclists at the Floralis Generica sculpture in the Plaza de Naciones Unidas, Buenos Aires.

country, near Bariloche, and the national parks every year.

Buenos Aires has more than 80 miles (130 kilometers) of cycle lanes and a public bicycle sharing system (Ecobici). Where there is no protected bike lane available, cyclists should stay on the right side of the road and keep an eye out for buses, particularly when they pull in and out at bus stops. You can register to use Ecobici bicycles via the app, which also provides details on the availability of bikes, addresses of pick-up stations, and maps of cycle lanes.

HEALTH AND INSURANCE

Pharmacists will dispense most medications, with many of them staying open all night. A list of pharmacies that are *de turno*—open all night, based on a rotation system—is normally displayed outside or on the window. Some medicines that might require a prescription in other countries may be sold over the counter in Argentina.

The state of the national health service in Argentina reflects the prevailing economic crisis and lack of investment. The medical profession in Argentina is still very highly regarded and of a high standard; however, this is particularly true in the private sector. Private medical insurance is more than strongly recommended. Unlike many countries, the private sector allows patients to make an appointment directly with a specialist rather than having to be referred by their family doctor, although the latter practice is still recommended.

WHERE TO STAY

Argentina has always been an attractive tourist destination, and the provision of accommodation has developed considerably over the last few years. There are options to meet all budgets, ranging from modest one- or two-star establishments to first-class international hotels. The major international chains are present, along with independent luxury hotels such as the Alvear Palace in the elegant area of Recoleta in Buenos Aires, one of the top hotels in Latin America. From modern towers and nineteenth-century French architecture to simple rural hotels or *hosterias*, there is no shortage of accommodation.

Accommodation in popular vacation destinations such as seaside and ski resorts is usually of a good standard. Huts and bungalows are very popular, particularly in the lake region in the south near the

Hotel Ilao Ilao in Bariloche, a popular city in Argentina's Patagonia region.

main ski resorts. They offer comfort and bucolic locations close to many national parks.

Residence inns (*apart-hotel*) are normally restricted to larger cities and are suitable for longer stays. Toward the lower end of the budget, bed and breakfast accommodation (*hostales*) is a good option for travelers wishing to explore local areas.

If you prefer a home away from home, Airbnb offers a wide choice of possibilities across Argentina.

SECURITY

Argentinian cities are not as dangerous as those in other Latin American countries. Unfortunately this relative safety has been affected by the economic crises of the last few years, the rise in the activity of drug cartels, and gang violence (particularly in Rosario), resulting in a sharp increase in both theft and violent crime. This is also the case in Buenos Aires, not only on account of its size and fast pace but also because of the widening gap between the rich and the poor. In a city where walking late at night once presented few problems, it is now advisable to take precautions. Be careful with belongings such as bags, purses, and cell phones, and try not to draw attention to yourself by carrying valuable objects, at least visibly.

It's sensible to avoid walking alone at night, particularly on dark, empty streets. Sadly, the number of violent crimes has soared in recent years, and robberies (often at gunpoint) and muggings have become more frequent. It is for this reason that it's advised to pay attention before boarding a taxi, and it's recommended that visitors stick to registered taxis.

Smaller cities and towns tend to be peaceful, safe places where life runs at a slower pace and people are hospitable, friendly, and welcoming. At times, the hospitality can be overwhelming as being a good host can sometimes mean accompanying visitors everywhere they go, all the time. If you prefer your privacy, a kind, diplomatic chat explaining that this is not necessary will suffice.

CHAPTER EIGHT

BUSINESS BRIEFING

BUSINESS CULTURE

Business practices in Argentina vary according to the region. The fast-moving businesspeople of Buenos Aires will be more vociferous and have developed a sense of polychronism that can disconcert the more methodical northern Europeans. Timetables will be juggled around to fit priorities. By contrast, their counterparts from smaller provincial towns will be more self-effacing and appear to be less emotional. They may find Porteños arrogant and slightly overbearing.

As in many other countries, who you know is more important than what you know. Knowing the right people to pull the right strings—a concept known as *acomodo* ("comfort")—can give the least likely candidate an excellent opportunity.

Because of the emotional and personal involvement Argentinians have with work—as opposed to the more rational and competence-driven approach found elsewhere—those who have been offered a job by virtue of their connections (*acomodados*) will tend to enjoy a certain amount of latitude.

Argentina, like many other Latin cultures, is very bureaucratic in its business approach. Expediency is not the foundation of business negotiations—in fact, the opposite is true. Argentinians like to take their time and believe that almost any aspect of a contract can be renegotiated unless there is a sudden change which merits urgency. In that case, Argentinians move very swiftly, are open to cutting corners, and can be quite creative in the process.

Like their Italian and Spanish ancestors, the Argentinians place more emphasis on personal relationships than on rules. They would rather do business with a friend than get down to the nuts and bolts of the legal aspects of a contract and neglect the personal side of the relationship. For visitors who come from a more formal context (in the Latin view, a colder approach), it is worth being prepared to consider the business scenario in terms of personal implications.

You will be more successful in business negotiations if you allow the time to build a relationship with your prospective partners and colleagues, where small talk on topics like football or current affairs will play a role, than if you try to stick to schedules and the letter of the law.

LEADERSHIP AND DECISION-MAKING

Argentinian business culture is generally one in which seniority is directly proportional to length of service, titles are extensively used, and decisions are made almost exclusively at the top level. Despite this, a shift toward a more achievement-oriented structure has become more prevalent as globalization gains ground, particularly in international organizations.

Many of these organizations are adopting a management and leadership style closer to that found in the USA, where a wider cross-section of the company can be involved in the decision-making process. However, as in many Latin and Mediterranean cultures, the system is generally quite hierarchical—the boss (*el jefe*) is still the boss, and he or she (although still mostly he) should be treated with the appropriate deference.

As Argentinian people are still very family oriented, bosses will often take a more lenient attitude toward their staffs' problems if those problems are family related. Unfavorable economic climates, sadly, have made organizations less ready to offer such leniency. The increased activity of trade unions has kept the senior management of many organizations in check. Strikes and picket lines are commonplace, as workers attempt to preserve their jobs.

Smaller Argentinian organizations typically have a little more latitude when it comes to employment policies and are less vulnerable to the effects of industrial action, although this is also changing as legislation starts to affect all areas of industry and commerce.

Superiors are still seen in a rather patriarchal light, and subordinates may turn to them for help in work-related and other issues. This is less evident in the large corporations but still very prevalent in smaller, family-run businesses.

TEAMWORK

The individualist mentality of the Argentinians is slowly giving way to a more cooperative approach. This is driven more by external market forces than by the Argentinians' own volition.

Teams have to be clearly directed if a successful outcome, or any outcome at all, is required. Argentinians as a people have traditionally been directed "from above," both politically and

professionally. Empowerment and autonomy should
be closely monitored, and sometimes teams might
require a gentle push in order to achieve results.

Argentinians tend to be professional in their
approach to work and are usually knowledgeable
when it comes to their own core competencies and
skills. However, you might end up with a team of
individual experts who will collectively struggle
to produce the synergy required for a result that
matches their expertise.

MEETINGS AND NEGOTIATIONS

Punctuality is expected in business meetings, and
a courtesy call if you are running late would not
go amiss. However, don't be surprised if the other
party does not reciprocate. It's not uncommon to
be kept waiting and in many cases, the more senior
the person, the longer you will be kept waiting. It's
advisable to reconfirm appointments a few days
prior to meeting.

Although many organizations require a certain
command of English as a prerequisite, the reality
is quite different when it comes to negotiating.
Even if your counterpart speaks relatively good
English, they might not feel comfortable enough to
conduct a transaction in English where the stakes

are higher than in, say, a presentation. On the other hand, the person on the Argentinian side with the right command of the language might not have the required seniority to negotiate or even take part. In these cases an interpreter is recommended, or ask your Argentinian counterpart for suggestions.

Once trust has been gained, mainly through small talk and perhaps some socializing, both parties will feel more at ease when it comes to discussing terms of business.

The Argentinians are less narrowly focused than other cultures (particularly the Americans and the Europeans) and negotiations might seem to go off at a tangent, with topics bordering on the irrelevant. It is perhaps best to let the meeting take its course, occasionally trying gently to get back on to the key issues if sidetracking has gone on too long. A hard sell approach is not recommended as it will be seen as pushy and neglecting the personal touch.

Presenting a series of clauses in a precise and logical manner is unlikely to fit the Argentinian model—Argentinians will consider the impact of the outcome from both a business and a personal point of view. The bottom line is not the be all and end all of business negotiations in Argentina.

Despite the lengthy nature of negotiations, a contract is only finalized when all terms have been agreed upon and the document has been signed.

Be prepared for last-minute changes and amendments; Argentinians can be tough negotiators.

PRESENTATIONS AND LISTENING STYLES

As in most of the rather emotional Latin cultures, the Argentinian speaking/listening pattern can be disconcerting to a visitor more accustomed to being listened to uninterruptedly, with time for questions at the end. Interruptions are likely to occur, so a preprepared script for a presentation will probably not work. Argentinians will listen, however, and although they might convey the impression that they are thinking about what they are going to say next rather than taking in what the presenter is saying, this is normally a misconception.

Very rigid and formal presentations are not recommended; the approach should be professional yet relaxed. Don't be surprised if not all the participants arrive on time. The presentation will normally start when the most senior person arrives, and still you might find latecomers trickling in after it has started. If a government contact, particularly at a high level, is involved, the meeting cannot start without their presence.

ETIQUETTE

It's still common practice to address someone senior or a new business acquaintance using the more formal *usted* (equivalent to the French *vous* or the German *Sie*), unless the other person insists that he or she be addressed as *vos*. If in doubt, choose the more formal option, which is normally used by calling people by their surname (without the use of Mr. or Mrs.) while still using the more formal register.

The exchange of business cards does not follow any formal protocol, and one might not always receive one in return.

During business meetings, the use of gestures should be controlled; it's likely that as the meeting progresses body language will relax. Eye contact should be maintained.

Office Dress and Etiquette

Argentinians place special emphasis on looks and appearance. They are stylish and fashionable, following the trends set by Italian and French fashion designers. Buenos Aires in particular has a very European outlook, and this is reflected in the way people dress. Dark suits for men and white blouses with suits or skirts for women are still the standard business attire. Casual Friday policies and an informal approach to business dress have only recently started to be introduced.

Ironically, this formality is counterbalanced by the extroverted nature and openness of the Argentinians. The formality of emails and letters can be effectively replaced by a friendly chat over a cup of coffee. Argentina is a country where the tools for relationship building are readily available and should not be disregarded if you want to speak to the right person.

BUSINESS AND SOCIAL MEALS

Gastronomy is a key part of the Argentinian lifestyle, both from a social and business perspective, and the standard of their food is something Argentinians are quite rightly proud of.

Business meals are commonplace and are normally held in the evening after working hours. If you are the host, payment should be arranged in advance where possible. Otherwise, you should insist on paying when the bill arrives. When summoning the waiter, do so by raising your hand, never by snapping your fingers. Although they are present on many tables, the use of toothpicks is ill advised, as is blowing one's nose at the table.

It's worth remembering that taxes on imported goods can be very high. Bear this in mind when

ordering imported drinks, particularly as a guest,
unless your host orders the drink in question.

GIFT GIVING

Argentina is not a country of lavish corporate gift
giving, but one where a favor or *gauchada*
is perhaps a preferred and more useful option.
Expensive gifts might be construed as bribes and
would put the receiver in an awkward position.

If you do give a gift, it's best to confine it to neutral
items. If you are given a gift, it should be opened
there and then, and appreciation shown. It is still
good practice to send flowers to your hostess if you
were invited for dinner. Pastries (*masas*), generally
served with coffee after a meal, or chocolates are
also suitable alternatives.

WOMEN IN BUSINESS

While Argentina is still a male-dominated culture,
women are gaining ground. Although they have
had political influence in the past, their standing in
both politics and business has become much more
visible over the last couple of decades. Women from
established wealthy families have occupied important
positions within the field of business and the arts.

Participants at the G20 Businesswomen Leaders Task Force meeting in Buenos Aires.

Foreign women should state their position, particularly the level of seniority within the company they represent, from the outset. They should not experience problems conducting business in Argentina as long as they remain professional in manner and dress and are sensitive to local norms.

CHAPTER NINE

COMMUNICATING

THE LANGUAGE

Spanish is the third-most widely spoken language in the world after Mandarin and English. However, the Castilian Spanish of Argentina differs widely in accent and to a certain extent in its grammar and vocabulary from that spoken elsewhere.

The European Spanish sound "z" (pronounced as "th" in thumb) is not used at all in Latin American Spanish from Mexico to Argentina. Argentinians pronounce the "ll" differently from all other Spanish-speaking countries. The "ll" in the word *lluvia* (the Spanish for rain), for instance, is pronounced as the "s" in "leisure," whereas in all other Spanish-speaking countries it would be pronounced as the "y" in "you." The same applies to the pronunciation of the letter "y." These two sounds are unmistakably Argentinian, although some Uruguayans, due to their proximity, have adopted them.

Another characteristic of the language, particularly in Buenos Aires, is the aspirated "s." This is used when the letter "s" precedes another consonant. Thus the "s" sound in words like *aspecto* (aspect), *fosforo* (a match, or the element phosphorus), and *estación* (station) sounds more like the "h" in "handbook."

There are several noticeably different accents within the country, the Spanish of the northern provinces sounding closer to that of the Paraguayans, and that of the northwest being reminiscent of the Spanish of Bolivia. People from Córdoba have perhaps the most distinctive accent to the untrained ear in Spanish, as they tend to lengthen their vowels in such a manner that it sounds almost as though they are singing.

Porteños tend to speak louder and faster than the rest of the population, in the belief that their speech is more sophisticated than those of the other provinces.

The general level of sound is much higher than it is in, say, the USA or the UK. It's not uncommon for visitors to think that people are shouting or raising their voice. This is not the case; if it were, the difference in body language and decibels would be a sure sign of ire even to those with no command of the language.

English is studied at school, but not in great depth and is not widely spoken outside certain circles. If you need to ask for directions in the street or communicate with a cab driver, a minimum knowledge of Spanish is recommended.

Learning Spanish

Spanish is spoken by over 500 million people worldwide. The differences between Argentinian Spanish and other forms of the language will not prevent Argentinian Spanish speakers from communicating with people from other Hispanic countries, in much the same way as a distinctive US accent will not impede communication with an Australian.

Spanish, irrespective of its accent, is a language that is rich in vocabulary, expressive in sound, and not as difficult to learn as other languages. There are some difficult points that take time to master, particularly as there are two forms of the verb "to be" (*ser* and *estar*).

There are several schools of Spanish for foreigners in Argentina. Daily life will provide learners with an ideal opportunity to learn, as the gregarious Argentinians will be happy to engage in conversation and will be more than indulgent if your tenses or your noun and article genders are not totally accurate.

A Few Language Tips

The Spanish alphabet consists of twenty-six letters, although the letter "w" is only used in words of foreign origin. (Some scholars also argue that the "*ch*" and the "*ll*" should be considered as separate letters.) Most Spanish nouns ending in "o" are masculine and most ending in "a" are feminine.

Spanish is pronounced as written, with vowel sounds being pure (i.e. one sound only per vowel, unlike English, where the "u" in "huge" consists of two sounds).

a Pronounced as in "have."

c Pronounced soft as in "city" before "e" or "i" and hard as in "can" before any other letter.

ch Always pronounced as in "chair."

e Pronounced as the "e" in "egg."

g Pronounced as the "ch" in "loch" before "i" or "e" and hard as in "go" in all other cases.

h This is a silent consonant with no exceptions. The aspirated "h" sound is not used for this letter in Spanish.

i Pronounced as the "ee" in "sheep."

j Pronounced as the "ch" in "loch."

ll Pronounced as the "s" in "leisure." This is one of the main sounds that differentiates Argentinian Spanish from most other forms of the language.

ñ Pronounced as in "new."

r "R"s are sometimes rolled and on occasions flicked. Double "r"s are always rolled.

s Pronounced as in "see." However, Argentinians tend to drop the "s" sound for an aspirated "h" sound, particularly when it appears in the middle of a word. The extent to which this is done varies regionally. Most people will pronounce the Spanish for "listen to me" (*escuchame*) with an aspirated "s."

t As in all Latin languages, the "t" is not aspirated; i.e.

it is formed by placing one's tongue slightly between the front teeth, thus avoiding the characteristic hissing English "t" sound.

u Always pronounced as the "oo" in "room."

v Strictly speaking, this is pronounced in the same way as in English. However, Argentinians tend to pronounce it in the same way as a soft "b"; i.e. by placing both lips together but still allowing some air to pass through them. It is not uncommon for people to refer to "v" as "*b corta*" ("short b") and "b" as "*b larga*" ("long b"), using the actual "b" sound in both cases!

y This is another characteristic Argentinian sound. Similar to the "ll" sound, it is pronounced as the "s" in "leisure."

z This is pronounced the same way as an "s". The characteristic European "th" (as in "thumb") sound is not used in Argentina, or indeed in other Latin American forms of the language.

As a result of slightly different grammar, some verbs are stressed differently than in European Spanish. The accent (´) placed above a word indicates that the syllable carries the stress (only one can appear in a word).

The second person singular and plural of verbs are where the difference in stress is normally found. While a Spanish person will say "*tu hazlo*," meaning "you do it," with a stress on the first syllable, Argentinians will say "*vos hacelo*" with the stress on the second syllable.

This being said, any foreigner in the process of learning the language will be taught the "classical grammar" used in Spain. However, the metalanguage (i.e. the language used to teach this so-called "classical grammar") will be Castilian Spanish. Saying "*tú tienes*" for "you have" instead of its Castilian equivalent of "*vos tenés*" will not only be forgiven but will also not impede communication in any way.

"*Che*": What Does It Mean?

This ubiquitous, informal, very singular three-letter word is used to convey a variety of messages. Its origin, according to some, dates back to the Guaraní language spoken in the northeast of Argentina and Paraguay, in which it meant "my" and "*che irú*," "my companion or mate." Its most common use is to informally call someone: "*Che, dónde vas?*" ("Hey, where are you going?") It can also be used to emphasize a question: "*Que hacés, che?*" (Loosely translated as "Hey, what are you doing?", also used as a very informal greeting.) It can even, with the right intonation, show emotions that range from slight disapproval to righteous indignation, normally pronounced with a long "*e*" sound at the end.

The use of "*che*" is one of the hardest aspects of the Argentinian language to teach in a formal educational setting. Its proper use can only be learned through practice and exposure to the language. The most important thing to remember is that it's used informally and shouldn't be used in business contexts, in much the same way that English speakers would avoid using the interjection "hey" in similar formal situations.

What's in a Nickname?

Ernesto Guevara, the famous leader of the Cuban revolution, was nicknamed "Che" by the Cubans as a result of his distinctive Argentinian accent and his frequent use of the word "*che*."

Slang

Lunfardo, as slang is called in Argentina, also varies regionally. Buenos Aires slang, normally associated with tango as the lyrics of that style of music feature many slang words, contains a high proportion of Italianized words. "*Laburo*" is the slang for "work" ("*lavoro*" in Italian), to name but one very frequently used example. While the younger generations have developed their own form of slang, the Italian ancestry so dominant in the population of Argentina, particularly Buenos Aires, continues to manifest itself through slang.

In other examples, "*piola*" is a widely used term that means "great" or "cool," while "*boludo*" can be used to mean "dude" or, in some contexts, "idiot."

A FEW USEFUL PHRASES

Hola Hello (also used when answering the phone)

Buen día/Buenos días Good morning (literally, Good day)

Buenas tardes Good afternoon

Buenas noches Good evening/Good night

¿Cómo estás? ¿Cómo andás? ¿Cómo te va? How are you? (informal)

¿Cómo le va? ¿Cómo está? How are you? (formal)

Por favor Please

Gracias Thank you

De nada You're welcome

Perdón Excuse me/Sorry (a simple "sori"—from the English "sorry"—is often heard)

¡Salud! Cheers/Bless you (as when someone sneezes)

Chau/Hasta luego/Adiós Goodbye

Mañana Tomorrow

Hoy Today

Ayer Yesterday

La semana que viene Next week

La semana pasada Last week

FACE-TO-FACE

Argentina is the place to go to for those who enjoy the art of conversation. Remember, the overall decibel level of the talkative Porteños is much higher than that of Northern Europeans. Conversations may sound agitated and hostile to the unaccustomed ear, but in most cases this is simply the characteristically Argentinian way of speaking, usually accompanied by quasi-choreographic displays of body language. In cafés, restaurants, and even public squares, particularly in Buenos Aires, it's likely you'll come across Argentinians engaging in some form of debate. Everyone claims to have the solution to the country's economic, political, or social problems, making debates of this nature quite intense, yet friendly.

Topics and Taboos

Argentinians are happy to criticize their own country quite vociferously but don't take well to outside criticism. Topics such as the South Atlantic War should be avoided; if asked your opinion on the war it is best to be as noncommittal as possible while showing sympathy toward those who perished during the conflict.

The subjects of Perón, his wives, government, or policies are best avoided. Care should be taken as there is no middle ground here—feelings on Perón, whether positive or negative, will be very strong. Admittedly more popular with the working classes, even idolized by many, he also has supporters among the better educated.

Argentinians do not like to be challenged and will tend to adopt a defensive attitude, while managing to reply with a smile on their face. Delving too deeply into the rationale of a particular piece of legislation or the "why" of the status quo is not advisable unless, of course, you know the other person quite well.

Other areas to be avoided, at least when talking to new acquaintances, are racism, religion, and other personal or sensitive topics such as the Nazi war criminals living in Argentina. These issues may be too close for comfort, and may elicit comments or opinions that are likely to offend visitors from more multicultural societies.

In line with Argentinians' pride in their European ancestry, comparisons with other Latin American countries should be avoided. This is particularly true of Brazil, where there is still a slight feeling of animosity, although perhaps more on behalf of the Brazilians, who see the Argentinians as arrogant and abrupt.

Silence

Most Argentinians don't feel particularly comfortable with silence. This is perhaps more true of city dwellers than those living in remote rural areas, however.

The Argentinian pattern of conversation is almost uninterrupted, giving the impression that people are already thinking about what to say next while you are talking to them. This fast pace of exchange is hard to keep up with at first, but most visitors will be given grace and their hosts will slow down the flow of their speech to accommodate them.

Swearing

Swearing has become more commonplace in
Argentina. While no swearing used to be heard
on radio and television, this has changed with the
arrival of democracy. Nevertheless, even in today's
more relaxed society, the use of coarse language by
younger Argentinians is frowned on by many of the
older generation. Swearing is still widely viewed as
unnecessary and as showing a lack of refinement,
and visitors are encouraged to avoid it.

Argentinian swear words tend to allude to one's
maternal ancestry, and although these are often used
inoffensively—perhaps to emphasize a feeling, not
always of anger or discontent—it will take time and a
certain amount of restraint to get used to this.

Humor

Argentinians are always ready for a good laugh,
generally at somebody else's expense. Their humor
is less subtle than British humor, which is often
not thought funny. Understatement is not part of
Argentinian humor, although situational visual
comedy is. Irony and wit are key elements in the
humor of Buenos Aires, which makes good use of
the richness of the region's language.

Argentinians are not very good when it comes to
laughing at themselves and would much rather pick on
a different group of people. The Spanish, notably the
Galicians (Gallegos), have historically been the butt

of many jokes. Sadly, the definition of Galicians has extended to anyone speaking with a European Spanish accent.

ETIQUETTE

Greetings

Men normally greet each other with a handshake and a slight nod of the head. Women may do the same, sometimes shaking hands with both hands and kissing each other on the cheek (once). This has become common among men, who will kiss each other on the cheek, although this is normally restricted to close friends and relatives. Once acquainted, men might hug each other (*abrazo*) too.

Handshaking between men and women is seen as quite formal. Instead, men and women usually kiss each other on the cheek when greeting. Don't be surprised if greeted in this way by a member of the opposite sex.

You or you?

Like many languages in the world, Spanish has two forms of the second person singular, which are selected according to how formally one has to address the other person.

It is worth mentioning one of the main differences in grammar between Argentinian Spanish (Castellano) and the language spoken in all other Spanish-speaking countries. While the informal variation of the second person is *tú* in all other countries, in Argentina it is *vos*.

Nowadays, particularly in shops and retail outlets, it is not uncommon for staff to address customers using the less formal register.

Punctuality

When invited to a meal, a reception, the theater, or a concert, you should arrive on time. However, for less formal social events like parties, arrival times are looser: guests are expected to arrive later than the stipulated time, to the extent that arriving on time could be considered impolite.

If punctuality is required, the time will be emphasized with the qualifying expression *en punto* (on the dot).

Body Language

You will realize almost immediately that the outgoing personality of the Argentinians is complemented by a rich-sounding language and very visible body language. It is usual for two parties to sit opposite each other and the host will, in many cases, usher the guest to their seat.

Argentinians tend to stand closer to each other when communicating. While this may make some visitors uncomfortable, avoid backing away as this will send the wrong signals. People also go in for much more physical contact—hugs, kissing, handshaking, and placing a hand on a person's back when inviting them in or asking them to go first are all ways that Argentinians like to communicate.

INTERNET AND SOCIAL MEDIA

As in most countries today, the Internet forms an important part of daily life in Argentina. In 2023, Internet penetration stood at 89.7 percent of the population and of those with Internet access (some 40 million people), 91 percent used at least one social media platform.

WhatsApp, followed closely by Facebook and Instagram, are the platforms most popularly used by Argentinians. "*¿Tenés WhatsApp?*" (Are you on WhatsApp?) will be the first question when trying to make any type of arrangement, be it personal or work-related. Facebook had 27.3 million Argentinian users in 2023, with 53 percent of its users women and 47 percent men. Instagram had 23.4 million users and is favored by younger people, and more women than men. Though both Instagram and Facebook are used commercially, sponsored content still lags behind that of other Latin American countries. TikTok had over 11 million users in Argentina aged 18 and above in 2023, Twitter had around 5.9 million, and Snapchat over 2 million.

THE PRESS

There is no shortage of newspapers in Argentina.
Every province has its own local newspaper in addition
to the main national press. The leading national
papers are *Clarín* (also the second most widely read
in the Spanish-speaking world), which has a liberal
center-right editorial stance, and *La Nación*, a popular
conservative daily. *Infobae* is a highly popular digital
news platform based in Argentina but with offices
throughout Latin America and in the US. *Ambito
Financiero* and *El Cronista Comercial* are the two most
popular financial papers. Newspapers published in
English include the digital *Buenos Aires Herald* and
Buenos Aires Times. Other useful online news sources
for those who don't speak Spanish include *Télam
English*, the English-language service of the National
News Agency of Argentina, and *The Bubble,* which
provides more magazine-style news and commentary.

TELEVISION AND RADIO

Television is an integral part of Argentinian life.
Eating in front of the TV and having it perpetually on,
whether or not it is being watched, is still common
practice in many households.

There are five VHF/UHF channels available:
Channel 13 (Artear), Channel 11 (Telefe), Channel 2

(America TV), Channel 9 (Libertad), and Channel 7 (RTA), the state television channel. Most films and foreign programs are dubbed (rather than using subtitles), unlike those shown in the cinema, where subtitles still prevail (see pages 122–123).

In addition to this, the satellite and cable-TV network extends to almost all the country, giving access to international channels such as the BBC and CNN.

There are many radio stations broadcasting in both AM and FM, with programs to suit every audience.

Television streaming services are available and widely used in Argentina, Netflix being the most popular with 5 million subscribers in 2023, followed by Disney+, HBO Max, Paramount+, and Amazon Prime. In June 2022 an Argentine thriller, *La Ira de Dios* (*The Wrath of God*), ranked amongst the five most widely watched films globally on Netflix.

MAIL

The main postal company is the Argentinian Post (Correo Argentino), which works reasonably well. There are other private companies such as Oca and Servicor who have branches across the country and provide reliable services.

Using standard delivery, a letter can take from ten to fifteen days from Argentina to the UK, and slightly less to the USA. Special delivery services and international courier companies like DHL and FedEx are widely available.

CELL PHONES AND SIM CARDS

The three main cell providers in Argentina are Claro, Personal, and Movistar, all of which have prepaid SIM card packages for short-term visitors. You can buy SIM cards on arrival at the airport, in official retail stores, or at the ubiquitous *kioskos*. In their official retail stores, Personal and Claro sell prepaid SIM cards and will register the SIM using your passport details, so don't forget to bring your passport along with you. Movistar retail stores do not currently sell or register prepaid SIM cards. If you buy a SIM card at a *kiosko*, you will need to do the activation yourself online.

To call cell phones in Buenos Aires you must dial the prefix 15. If phoning an Argentine cell phone from abroad, 15 need not be included but a number 9 must be included between the country code and the city code, e.g. 0054 9 11 1234 5678.

The international dialing code for Argentina is 54, the code for Buenos Aires is 11, and all numbers start with a 4. Long-distance area codes vary according to the region: 1 for Buenos Aires and the surrounding area, 2 for the south of the country, and 3 for the north of the country.

The prefix for long-distance calls is 0, followed by

the area code, and for international calls the prefix is
00 followed by the country code.

EMERGENCY SERVICES

Police: 911 or 101

Ambulance: 107

Fire: 100

The Tourist Police in Buenos Aires offers assistance in
English and is available 24 hours. If using a foreign mobile
phone, dial 0054 9 11 5050 9260/3293. If phoning from a
local telephone, dial 5050 9260/3293.

CONCLUSION

Argentina sometimes seems like a European country
that has somehow been misplaced in South America.
It is a huge and appealing country, whose importance
in the global economy as a producer of food has
enabled it to survive the direst of economic crises,
and is waiting behind the scenes for the right moment
to reveal its potential and perhaps relive its former
glory as one of the richest countries in the world.

The Argentinians never cease to astound
visitors with the sophistication of the Porteños
and the candidness and laid-back style of the rural
population. Argentina is still a place where, despite

ongoing difficulties, friendship is a key ingredient in getting things done. It is a country that has lived for today and looks as though it will continue to do so, its people having developed an art of extemporization that is probably second to none. The Argentinians' identity is still very Southern European, and their exuberant way of life will charm and engage even the most reticent and self-effacing visitors.

From a business perspective, the latitude that Argentinians allow themselves when it comes to punctuality and the amount of small talk that normally precedes getting down to business is counterbalanced by their openness and hospitality, and a wish to show the best they have to offer.

The Argentinians are a vibrant and resilient people, proud of their success in recovering from repressive dictatorial regimes, and whose joie de vivre and generosity of spirit can be contagious. They will be happy to teach you about their country, their people, their traditions, and their rich and colorful language. Here is a society where making friends is part of daily life, and where becoming part of that way of life will prove to be an exciting, enriching, and unique experience.

FURTHER READING

Albiston, I.; Brown, C.; Clark, G.; Egerton, G.; Grosberg, M.; Kaminski, A.; McCarthy, C; Skolnick, A. *Lonely Planet Argentina 12 (Travel Guide)*. Lonely Planet Publications, 2022.

Bracken, J. *¡Che Boludo! A Gringo's Guide to the Argentines*. Editorial Caleuche, 2014.

Chatwin, B. *In Patagonia*. Vintage Classics, 2017.

DK Eyewitness Argentina. DK Eyewitness Travel, 2017.

Esposto, R. *Lonely Planet Latin American Spanish Phrasebook & Dictionary*. Lonely Planet, 2018.

Goñi, Uki. *The Real Odessa: How Perón Brought the Nazi War Criminals to Argentina*. London: Granta Books, 2003.

Guevara, E. *The Motorcycle Diaries: Notes on a Latin American Journey*. New York: Seven Stories Press, 2021.

Lewis, Colin M. *Argentina: A Short History*. Oxford: Oneworld, 2002.

Nouzeilles, G. and Montaldo, G. *The Argentina Reader: History, Culture, Politics*. Durham and London: Duke University Press, 2002.

Richardson, J; Cosen-Binker, L.; Diamondstein, C.; Caviezel, P.; Stern, E. *¡Hola Buenos Aires! Everything You Need To Know Before Moving To Buenos Aires*. Buenos Aires: University Women's Club, 2012. (Includes information on where to rent or buy a house and how, where to send children to school, to whom to call in an emergency, and includes a Spanish glossary.)

Stephenson, S. *Understanding Spanish-Speaking South Americans: Bridging Hemispheres*. Intercultural Press, 2003.

USEFUL APPS & WEBSITES

Communication and Socializing

BA Wifi provides details on over 1,200 free Wi-Fi hotspots in Buenos Aires.

Buenos Aires Expats Website where expats share experiences and help each other out (baexpats.org).

Porteño Spanish teaches you the peculiarities of the Spanish spoken in Buenos Aires.

Tinder, **Badoo**, and **Bumble** are Argentina's most widely used dating apps.

WhatsApp Argentina's number one messaging app.

For Events in English in Buenos Aires See the Argentine-British Community Council website (abcc.org.ar), University Women's Club (uwcba.org), and Suburban Players (thesuburbanplayers.com).

Travel and Transportation

BA Ecobici Buenos Aires bike sharing app. Though sometimes rather rickety, the bicycles are free to use on weekdays.

BA Taxi Hail-a-ride app for use in Buenos Aires.

BA Turismo Official city app for tours, museums, sights, and more.

Cómo Llego Buenos Aires route-planning app.

Cabify and **Uber** are the two most used ride-hailing apps in Argentina's main cities.

Despegar is the most popular site for purchasing flight tickets.

Trenes Argentinos For train schedules.

Food, Shopping, and Entertainment

Argentine Wine App Helpful info on the country's many wines.

The Fork Good app for booking a table at restaurants and offers discounts on reservations made through the app. Many of the top restaurants manage their bookings through their own websites.

LightsOut Nightlife app (currently Android only).

Mercado Libre Shop new and second-hand items on South America's most popular shopping platform.

Mercado Pago For online payments and money transfers.

USEFUL APPS

Milonga Hoy For tango classes, perfomances, and more.
Pedidos Ya Argentina's most widely used food delivery service.
Ticketek.com.ar For concert tickets.
Rappi Comprehensive food and grocery delivery service.
Restorando Research restaurant options in Buenos Aires and book a table.

INDEX

Acknowledgments

This book is dedicated to Juan, Brenda, and Aileen, who always listen. A special thanks to Silvana Piga, Lorraine Sandford, Janet Bruce, Phyllis Barrantes, and Lucy Santamarina.